LOVED &

RESTORED

JOHN McCREEDY

LOVED &
RESTORED

THE STORY OF NAOMI

AMBASSADOR
INTERNATIONAL
Celebrating Forty Years of Getting the Word Around

Loved and Restored

Paperback: ISBN: 978-1-62020-895-3
eBook: ISBN: 978-1-62020-430-6

Printed in the UK
Front cover design by Esther Kotecha

Ambassador International
Emerald House
411 University Ridge, Suite B14
Greenville, SC 29601
www.ambassador-international.com

Ambassador Books and Media
The Mount
2 Woodstock Link
Belfast, BT6 8DD, Northern Ireland, UK
www.ambassadormedia.co.uk

For Margaret Hillis (Auntie Margaret)

Because of her continued unconditional love and support throughout the writing of this book and within my own life, she's helped restore me in more ways than I can remember.

A great gift from God!

Contents

Foreword

I first met John about eight or nine years ago, at an event UCB was hosting at Whitewell Tabernacle in Belfast. Over the years, we kept in touch and I have always thought of John as a man 'with a heart for the Kingdom'. It is clear that he loves people and has a passion for seeing broken believers restored to all that God wants them to be. It is a passion we have in common.

Many years ago, my wife and I lost our 18 month old son, Jamie, to cot death. In years to come, we would also lose a grandson and we have also seen critical illness affect many members of our family. I remember after one experience, when our daughter-in-law was gravely ill in a coma, I was reminded of a verse in Psalm 92, 'The righteous shall flourish like a palm tree.' As I studied this verse, I discovered that Palm trees are designed to withstand severe tropical storms. When the storm comes, they don't break with the ferocity of the wind, they bend along with the storm and the rain. On the outside, it might look as though they are breaking, but they are actually just bending.

Thank God, our daughter-in-law made a full recovery, but as a family, having gone through many storms of our own, we know what it is to be broken, to feel as though we cannot take any more pain or heartache. But we also know how it feels to 'bend in the storm' and to be restored by a miracle-working God.

John's colourful re-telling of the story of Naomi and the many trials she went through, is a powerful reminder that we serve a God who is still in the business of restoration. So often Scripture hints at what Biblical characters might have felt and experienced during the hardest trials of their lives, but we will not fully know what happened, until we get to Heaven. That is why Loved and Restored, with John's account of what might have happened, is an important book for people who are hurt and who are suffering.

There is a clear reminder through the life of Naomi (and her daughter-in-law Ruth) that even though we may walk through the darkest of times, God (as he says in his Word) will never leave us or forsake us. We might not always understand His plan, but we can always be assured that He does have one.

So, if you have picked up this book and are feeling battered by the storms of life, I pray that you will feel revived by the re-telling of this ancient story and that as you turn to God's Word, you will find answers, hope and healing.

David L'Herroux
CEO United Christian Broadcasters

Special thanks...

To my wife Louise, who has known joy and pain but always remains the same. Thank you for your powerful prayers, faithfulness and unconditional love.

And special thanks to Robin Watson, a real brother and friend, for inspiring and encouraging me to write this book. Your overall contribution has proved invaluable.

To the very talented Esther Kotecha for producing a beautiful front cover.

To Mark Linton and the team at Ambassador International for believing in the potential of this book and displaying the determination and compassion to see men and women restored.

To John (Jay) Henderson for finding a quiet place for me to write much of this book and providing free tea and coffee and tons of love.

And finally, special thanks to Naomi, someone I've lived and breathed for several years now. I hope you enjoy her story.

While this book is based on the Biblical account of the story of Naomi in the book of Ruth, I must also point out that this manuscript is also my dramatisation of what might have happened back in those Old Testament times. To freshen the story and make it relevant to our current generation, I've added in some characters and events and conversations which I imagine might have taken place. The book is nevertheless biblically based concentrating on the book of Ruth, found in the Old Testament and sandwiched between Judges and the First book of Samuel. Naomi is the star of the show, and I hope you are blessed by her incredible story.

Introduction

The Mountains were beautiful in the background, and the barley was in its season.

A warm, summer breeze was blowing. David tightened his sling and aimed at the tree. His shot was so far off target he dropped his head in disgust. His grandfather saw the anguish of his son and hurried towards him.

David noticed him coming and tried again, but with a similar result. Again, he shook his head. What must his grandfather think?

"You've lost your concentration, son."

"I can't do it, Grandfather. People are expecting far too much from me. They forget that I am just a shepherd boy and nothing else."

David sighed and strolled gently down the hill towards the end of the garden, still agitated and fiddling with the sling in his hand. His grandfather followed him down and placed his staff on the wall where David had just sat down.

The old man put his arm around his grandson and said softly: "I remember someone who overcame the most incredible odds and made such a remarkable recovery people still refer to her today. It's a gripping tale of hope, faith and most of all trust. When we can't understand what God is doing in our lives the qualities of faith, confidence and trust are essential."

"When did all of this take place, Grandfather?"

"It all began many years ago during the time of the Judges. It was a period in history where corruption was evident, and when the famine came upon Israel, many families decided to escape their plight by moving to the neighbouring country of Moab."

"Isn't that a pagan nation, Grandfather?"

"Yes, and not just pagan, the people of Moab were bitter enemies of our country Israel. Anyway, it was a futile move for most, because Moab proved to be no better than Israel."

"In what way was it no better, Grandfather?"

"The famine arrived there, too, and the people suffered just as much for there was no rain."

"Is that all?"

David's grandfather smiled. "Oh no, young man, that's not the end of this story, not by a long, long way. Would you like to hear more?"

"Yes please, Grandfather, keep going, I'm listening."

One

A Child of His Time

"In those days there was no king in Israel. Everyone did what was right in his own eyes." (Judges 21:25)

Elimelech had been restless for months. Only he knew the true extent of his anguish. His personal life had imploded, and things were at an all-time low. Struggling in his faith and seeking a way out, he couldn't tell a soul, not even his godly wife, Naomi.

A severe famine had struck Israel leaving Elimelech and his fellow countrymen in crisis. The earnest prayers of this once devoted religious man had yielded no fruit, and he felt personally responsible. He'd grown tired of shepherds, sheep, and goats; and wary of an unknown God who, in his eyes, wasn't meeting the needs of him, his family, or his nation. Come to think of it, what an embarrassment for someone like Elimelech whose very name denoted "My God is King"— yet where was this king when he needed him most?

Carrying what seemed like the "weight of the world" on his shoulders, he'd tried everything to solve the problem, but found no solution.

In short, his faith wasn't working, and he knew it.

Is there anything worse than religion without results?

What is more discouraging than an expectation without realisation?

A precarious form of existence, it had been Elimelech's reality for some time. Daily he'd return home to Naomi, disheartened and with the same tale of woe, until one day something snapped. Months of frustration finally gave way to anger.

Elimelech couldn't keep silent any longer.

"There's no work and no bread in Israel, Naomi. If things remain like this, the roof will cave in on us. We have to do something; we have to leave this place — and quickly."

"Not again, Elimelech. How many times have I heard this?

"It's different this time, our situation is dire. Israel can't help us. God isn't even helping us. When was the last time we enjoyed a decent meal?"

Naomi listened intently to her husband like she always did. An energetic and spirited individual, she was gentle but tough — a woman with a deep-rooted faith in God.

Her strength was God's strength.

Regarding spiritual matters, she would make a formidable opponent for anyone, even her anxious and discouraged husband. Unlike Elimelech, Naomi had cultivated the habit of persistent prayer. Where others would have given up, Naomi kept going until heaven responded. Making random decisions, therefore, without the permission of her God was not her standard way of life. It was how Elimelech used to be until restlessness entered his tired soul causing him to want to abandon his devotional times and their homeland.

Naomi, however, quickly reminded her husband how everything they knew and related to was in Israel. It was who they were. Israel was in their soul. She didn't want to lose her religious identity in a foreign land, especially Moab? But Elimelech had other ideas.

"Protest all you like, Naomi, I've had it with this place. I'm tired of watching our crops fail. I'm weary not being able to make ends meet. Every day I go to work with a heavy heart, and nothing appears to be changing. God gives us a choice and I've made up my mind; we're moving to Moab and soon."

The meagre scraps and poor way of life they were experiencing at that time was so vastly different to how things used to be. For example, before the arrival of the famine, Naomi and Elimelech had enjoyed a blessed and happy life in Bethlehem, Judah. Traditional and prosperous, they were committed Hebrews, influential and famous people in Canaan.

Elimelech, an Ephrathite of an ancient noble line, was considered to have been quite prominent in Israel, belonging to a distinguished family, being a brother of Salmon, prince of Judah, who married Rahab, mother of Boaz.

Strikingly, despite the best efforts of both Jewish and Christian writers to prove otherwise, the Bible doesn't attempt to smooth over the awkward fact that Boaz's mother, Rahab had been a harlot. Instead, she found mercy with God to the extent where she became part of God's covenant. While most people may attempt to hide the more embarrassing details of their family history, the Bible and Jesus displayed them openly. The most revered members of Christ's ancestry were all guilty of unspeakable crimes: Jacob was a thief, Solomon an idolater, David, a killer. Tamar was a temptress, Ruth a foreigner, Bath-Sheba an adulteress whose devoted husband was murdered by the king to cover up their sin, while Mary was a young girl whose unexpected (yet divinely appointed) pregnancy certainly raised more than a few eyebrows.

The ancestry of Christ is, thus, proof that with God, anyone can find mercy and acceptance. It reminds us how God can graft into His family whoever He chooses. The outsider can become an insider. Those who are written out can get written in. God's covenant grace is no respecter of persons. It can visit any tribe or tongue; it can rescue and restore any broken life, even the life of someone like Rahab. Man's extremity is frequently God's opportunity. Of course, once we consider how God changed the lives of many disreputable individuals, it is impossible to ignore the grace of God, the goodness of the cross and the kindness of Jesus!

Elimelech and Naomi had always been used to God's goodness but then famine cruelly struck Israel giving Elimelech the disturbing thought to migrate to the ungodly country of Moab, which lay east of the Dead Sea.

In those days, Elimelech and Naomi had two sons, Mahlon and Chilion, and they all lived during the rule of the Judges, similar to the period when everyone did that which was right in his own eyes, a time referred to as "Israel's Dark Ages."

The book of Ruth depicts such days, but its author and the time of writing are unclear. Scholars have failed to agree in relation to who wrote the book of Ruth, nor about when it was written. Some believe Samuel may have been the author to introduce Kingship in Israel and the family line of David, the great King. Others feel it was penned in the post-exilic period, when leaders like Ezra and Nehemiah were endeavouring to recreate national identity.

Regardless of which era it was birthed, however, it took place amidst a selfish and hedonistic generation, and even Naomi's husband, Elimelech, seemed susceptible to the apostasy around him.

A Torah observing Jew for many years, somewhere along the way he lost sight of his faith and God, preferring instead to do his own thing. A child of his time, he sensed provision in Moab, a new start and a safe place to live; an opportunity not to be missed!

What could be better, in fact? No more lack! No more begging for leftovers, something he'd religiously kept from his concerned wife, Naomi.

Elimelech had already passed the point of advice and counsel, having dismissed his well-meaning and concerned friends, many of whom had privately begged him to reconsider his plan. Two leading elders had tried desperately to talk Elimelech out of the move but without success. One of them even got down on his knees but to no avail.

"You need to carefully consider this rash decision Elimelech, especially the prospect of moving your family to Moab. Think about it, you're not getting any younger my friend and how will you find work in a heathen country. No one will hire you and your prospects are bleak."

"I appreciate your concern brethren, but it's not a rash decision, trust me. I've been planning this for some time. The prospects are better than this place. Nothing ever changes here, and the truth is I'm done both mentally and physically."

"You will be missed here in Israel. You are part of the fabric, Elimelech."

"I value your sentiments my dear brethren, but I'm not the man I was. If ever there is a time to jump ship, I believe this is it."

"You've definitely made up your mind, brother?"

"I've made up my mind."

"So we can't persuade you?"

"Nothing will persuade me. I'm sorry, it's time to leave!"

Deep down, however, Elimelech knew the solution to his misery — accept the pleas of his brethren and stay and allow God to solve the crisis in his nation and personal life, which, of course, would take immense trust, but trust was in short supply.

Instead, Elimelech seemed more prone to an inner voice challenging him to risk everything and leave Israel behind. Moab appeared to be working for others; why not him?

Besides, it was cowardly to stay put when a genuine opportunity was in front of him.

Naomi, too, sensed his dogged determination to abandon their nation of birth and it frightened her. There was no give in her husband, none of his usual softness, and no willingness to bend. Just colossal stubbornness she hadn't observed previously.

Just as he'd been stubborn with his brethren, he was stubborn with her. By Jewish culture, Naomi had always respected her husband and followed his leading, but surely a move from Israel to Moab was a step too far?

What if his decision was indeed rash and of the flesh?

What if things go pear-shaped?

What if it's not of God?

What then?

Their differing approaches to their faith, nation, and life, in general, reveal Naomi more as a woman of strength and loyalty; Elimelech as a weak and carnal man.

Previously, it appears Elimelech had believed the Word of God and obeyed it. He even rose to prominence in his province as a respected elder; until he traded the mighty power of the spirit for human weakness and fleshly gain which always leads to bad decision making.

Like Adam, who once walked with God in the garden before becoming separated from His Creator, Elimelech chose a similar road.

Was he wrong, though? Poverty had shattered his peace and altered his outlook on life, so in many respects he had a point, yet something else was motivating this ordinarily measured man to make uncharacteristic decisions.

Suddenly he appeared content to trust more in his own judgement than in God's.

All too aware of this, his wife watched as his personality altered and his patience ran out. Lack of provision had provoked within Naomi's husband pride, pragmatism and strong-headedness. Fed up living on the breadline, and longing for the more beautiful things in life, the once-soaring and robust faith of Elimelech had crumbled, and his frustration had spilt over. Not Naomi.

She remained resolute to their faith, refusing to give up without a fight to the end:

"Please, I beg you, Elimelech, pray about this. Israel is our home; there's nothing out there. God is good and, if we continue to trust Him, He will come through for us."

"God has forsaken us, Naomi."

"That's because people like you. Elimelech, refuse to believe God. You can't just do your own thing and uproot us because you're not prepared to wait on the promises of God. Have you forgotten that we are children of the most high God?"

"I>m sick of waiting, Naomi. That's all we seem to do is wait, wait, and wait. Remember how my mother always said; "The Lord helps those who help themselves."

"Where does it say that in scripture, Elimelech?"

"Fair enough, but where is God in Israel, Naomi? We've no food anymore and can't just sit here until we die. If we don't act now, we will go under."

"They that wait upon the Lord increase in blessings, not diminish Elimelech."

"I know, I know, Naomi, but there's a thing called reality and practicality. What about the monthly bills? How do you expect me to pay them? It's all right for you. You lie snoring at night, while I'm sweating over these matters."

"I lie snoring, Elimelech, because I trust in God, not in myself or mere mortals. Believe me; there's nowhere like Bethlehem, my dear husband. We are better remaining poor for the present and in the will of God, stretched in our faith but secure in God's promises than rich elsewhere and lose our reputations and spirituality altogether.

"Stop, Naomi and listen to me. I've told you: I've had it with Israel. The people are always moaning. We're not appreciated, and I'm tired of rejection and poverty. I've made up my mind, we've suffered enough. Everything has a season. It's time we thought of ourselves and made something happen. We're leaving, and that's the end of it."

While the Bible remains mainly silent about much of Elimelech's early life, Jewish history is not silent. It records how Elimelech was unhappy with his people because they were critical of their leaders. The people rejected him, so this caused Elimelech to refuse them and retaliate by going to live in the country of Israel's bitter enemies. One of the great men and authorities in Israel regarding his position, Elimelech appears to have lacked the character to go with it. According to Jewish legend, his deeply wounded spirit prompted him to take the unusual decision to turn his back on his birthplace and reside in the ungodly land of Moab.

What on earth would cause him to do such a thing?

As highlighted earlier, his name meant "My God is King", which presents Elimelech as a "man of faith", but another rendering of his name in Jewish record is known as "Kingship is due to me", indicating he may instead have been a man with a spirit of entitlement.

By the grace of God, kingship eventually came from the descendants of Elimelech, kingship was always in his blood, but it's significant that he never managed to become King of Israel.

Those who feel a sense of entitlement will never achieve as much as those who are truly grateful for everything they receive from a benevolent God.

For whatever reason he left Israel, the enemy managed to convince this pillar of the community to risk everything and throw utter caution to the wind literally. That said, we know that his family in Bethlehem faced starvation, so it's not unreasonable either to assume this may have left him with no other choice than to follow the example of Abraham and Jacob, who swapped Canaan for Egypt due to famine (Genesis 46:1).

Nonetheless, why did he elect to go to Moab and not Egypt like Abraham and Jacob?

Moab was closer and thought to be slightly more at peace with Israel at the time of the Judges, but she was no friend of Israel and besides, none of this appeased the apprehensive Naomi, a woman out of her mind with worry.

"Elimelech, listen to me," she continued. "You know I love and respect you, and I want what's best for you and our family. I understand you've made up your mind, but I don't want to leave Israel. It's far too big a risk, and we've two young boys to think of."

"That's why we're moving, Naomi. I am thinking of the two boys. Do you want them growing up in a place like this where God appears to have gone, and we've hardly a scrap of food on the table? Be real!"

"It may be so, Elimelech, but we don't know a single soul in Moab. Have you even considered this? And another thing, where will we worship? It's a pagan land while Israel has been our home from birth. We are unfamiliar with another culture. Have you even contemplated this?"

"That's all you're worried about, isn't it — worship, God, and tradition? There's more to life than God's temple Naomi, and one of those things is feeding our bellies."

"Strange how you've forgotten so quickly about the bread of life — the Word of God, Elimelech."

"I've never heard of anyone who has eaten a bible for dinner, Naomi and felt nourished, have you?»

"Amusing, Elimelech, hilarious and at a time like this!"

Naomi's disappointment was clear. She couldn't figure out why her husband felt so unsettled and obligated to leave their fellow countrymen in such a hurry, but she knew he was serious. She'd always got her way previously, but not on this matter.

Leaving?

Tomorrow?

Those words penetrated her heart and soul. She would barely have time to say goodbye to her family and friends, people she'd known and loved all of her life. And, to make matters worse, they were heading to a country which worshipped idols.

Surely Naomi had a point?

Why would a Torah observing Jew like Elimelech want to bring his family to live amongst the idolaters of a foreign nation? Couldn't he just as quickly have settled in other more easily reached regions rather than having to undertake an arduous journey through steep terrain to the land of Moab?

In the most tragic manner conceivable, Naomi would one day receive the answer to such a question and reap the dreadful consequences of her husband's decision. For now she was duty bound to follow her husband's wishes. She couldn't help wonder what was going on in his troubled mind, although she'd been aware of his restlessness in Israel for some time.

For months she hadn't heard him utter a single prayer, not even a kind word. Israel had become a place of despair to Elimelech, and he became desperate for a change at all costs. He kept hearing about how much better things were in Moab, and he wanted a slice of it for him and his family. In some ways he'd been institutionalised for years which had produced inquisitiveness regarding the outside world, like he was being driven away from all things familiar by a superior force.

For some time, Naomi had also witnessed her husband neglect the Hebrew customs and laws. Even his sons and friends became aware of his indifference. There was no passion, pride or desire within Elimelech to pursue a faith that had grown cold. Buried deep beneath the surface of this man's heart was a spirit of restlessness, a secret he'd hidden from just about everyone; daily torture he'd wrestled with regularly leaving him fearful, vulnerable and uncomfortable.

There were other questions for Naomi: Why was a heathen nation like Moab more blessed than Israel — a country that didn't even believe in Jehovah God? Why was a God-rejecting foreign land suddenly the one flowing with milk and honey while Israel famished?

Why was there rain in Moab, but not Bethlehem?

These became searching questions for both of them. Notwithstanding; Naomi and her generation would come to learn how God's love is merciful to us all. He makes the sun to rise on the evil and the good and sends rain on the just and the unjust. His love for His creation is impartial. While Israel is undoubtedly unique to God, the birthplace of His very own Son, while it is a light unto many nations and has a prophetic place in scripture, clearly, therefore, God loves all nations.

People everywhere, without exception, experience times of trial and trouble. Israel herself has never been exempt from this trouble or hardship, a rule which also applies to God's people. In the same way that down the years, Israel has endured its share of famine, the people of God have known their fill of religious persecution, too.

A lack of rain and, insects destroying food supply and crops, frequently caused starvation in Israel and, throughout other parts of the Middle East and even today; many of God's people experience lack and hardship. Such adversity caused Elimelech to carry out his threats to up sticks and leave and to trade Bethlehem — the house of bread — for Moab, a pleasure-seeking country named after the unfaithful Lot.

It was soon obvious to faithful Naomi that her husband couldn't be convinced to stay. He no longer wanted to suffer in Israel with his brethren. He was tired of poverty, pain, and financial pressure and desired a new start for his wife and family. Moab may have seemed a more blessed and prosperous nation, but in reality, it was a spiritually bankrupt region, which would ultimately bring Elimelech and his family immense tragedy.

Still, Naomi made one final, final attempt to persuade her rebellious husband to see sense and wait. Determined Naomi fought to the bitter end to remain in Israel.

"Are you sure we're leaving, Elimelech? Have you fully made up your mind? Remember, this is the biggest decision we've ever had to make."

"Naomi, I'm sure, trust me everything will work out fine. Sometimes in life, you need to follow your instincts."

"Follow your heart, maybe, but never your instincts, Elimelech."

"Naomi, I'm happy with the decision to try something new, and I'm convinced all should be okay. If not, we can always return here at a later date."

"I hope you're right because you've got more than one person to think of in this situation and what if you get it wrong, Elimelech?"

"Don't be so negative, Naomi. The world is our oyster, and the sky's the limit. Learn to embrace the future and life. We've reached a major crossroads: It's now or never! Do or die! Stretch or starve!"

His beautiful and diplomatic wife couldn't stall her husband's hasty plan, no matter how hard she tried.

There was just no talking to him.

His course was set.

Elimelech was a man on a mission.

Famine, fear and a failing faith had won the day.

Two

Far-Off Fields

"And Elimelech Naomi's husband died, and she was left,
and her two sons" (Ruth 1:3)

The drought had slowly crippled Israel forcing the inhabitants elsewhere. For some time the country had lost its invincibility. Once a beacon of hope and strength to other nations, Israel was struggling, and the residents were deserting in their droves, helped by a well-established route to Moab crossing the Jordan just north of the Dead Sea.

Similar to Jacob's time when news spread to Canaan that *"there was grain for sale in Egypt,"* (Genesis 42:1 ESV) news quickly reached the natives in Bethlehem that times were more prosperous in Moab.

When it comes to financial survival in life, nothing reveals character quicker than a crisis!

Starvation is no laughing matter!

The loyalty and even patriotism of the most committed people can go out the window and for understandable reasons. In such circumstances, a man with a wife and children is often obliged to make harsh decisions as was the case with Elimelech and Naomi, required to pack up and get out of Bethlehem or stay where they were and die.

Having chosen to leave Bethlehem, Elimelech may well have believed he'd only acted like any good husband and father in a similar situation — he took his wife and family away from the famine-stricken area to a more prosperous place. He removed his loved ones from danger and from what he perceived as a lack of material and spiritual blessing to a more affluent region. Notwithstanding; it remained for the unfortunate Naomi to enlighten her two sons they were leaving the land of their birth, Israel, a task she didn't relish.

"I've something to share with you boys, and I need you to understand."

"Is everything okay mother? You're not sick, are you?" enquired an anxious Mahlon.

"I'm fine; it's not about me, it's about all of us. Your father has decided we're not staying in Israel. He says the famine is too severe and it's in our best interests to move to Moab."

"Are you sure, mother? Have you both thought this through?" added Chilion.

"I'm not happy about it, but your father insists, so hurry up, boys, pack your things; we're leaving for Moab tomorrow."

"Tomorrow?

"You can't be serious, Mother?"

"Moab? How far is that?"

"It's about sixty miles from Israel, Mahlon, but we may have to travel further. The famine is mainly to blame. Quickly get your stuff and let's go."

The terrain from Israel to Moab didn't make the terrifying move any more comfortable. Tired and hungry they would eventually reach their destination some days later, filled with trepidation. Picture the turmoil experienced by Elimelech and Naomi following their entrance to the unfamiliar nation of Moab? Before leaving Israel, Elimelech had mortgaged his property back in Bethlehem, and now here they were arriving on foreign soil with nothing.

The aim seems to have been *"to live for a while in the country of Moab"* (Ruth 1:1 NIV), probably until the famine was over. The fact that Elimelech still owned property in Bethlehem makes it likely he had genuinely anticipated returning home at some point, but our best laid plans don't always materialise. Certainly, the usual feelings of sadness, loneliness, and extreme vulnerability would have set in as they came to terms with the magnitude of the sudden change in their lives — a culture shock none of them had encountered before.

Culture upheaval today is unprecedented and similar; it's a daily reality for millions of people who relocate freely or are forced to move to foreign shores. Anyone who has lived, studied, or even travelled extensively to another nation knows the effects of culture shock. Everything is unfamiliar; weather, landscape, language, food, dress, social roles, values, customs and communication. Business is conducted in a way that can be hard to understand; the stores are opened and closed at unfamiliar hours. The smells, sounds and tastes are unusual, and, in many cases, people can't communicate with the locals — not even to buy a loaf of bread.

Elimelech and Naomi would have gone through all this strangeness, but where they would have noticed the biggest difference would have been in their religious lives. Continually comparing Moab with Bethlehem, the differences would have been striking. Elimelech attempting to extol the material virtues of Moab; Naomi harping on about how much better it was in their beloved Bethlehem. Deeply unhappy, and for the sake of her husband and family, Naomi desperately tried to make a go of things. Moab wasn't her home, and it never would be, culturally or spiritually. On the contrary, it was a worldly, ungodly, and idolatrous dwelling, a place far removed from the peace she would have known in Bethlehem.

Historically, Moab and Ammon were born to Lot and Lot's elder and younger daughters respectively, in the aftermath of Sodom and Gomorrah. It was a heathen nation, and a people whose relationship with Judah is characterised by a deep and historical hostility.

Naomi, in particular; would have become extremely frightened as she and her family began to experience an unpredictable future, culture and different world from the one she had left behind.

Contrast this to Elimelech who appeared content to start over in a land where worship of the true and living God was discouraged — a fact hard to comprehend given his strong religious upbringing in Israel.

It wasn't long before the heart of this devout Israelite forgot the Promised Land and the religious customs and society he knew. His sons knew no example to follow, had no mentor to learn from, and no spiritual father to emulate. They became uneducated about the history of Israel, the Law of Moses, and the ways of God. Instead, from here on, they lost track of who they were and eventually would become like the Moabites. Such a dramatic change of cultural and religious expression may readily explain why Elimelech's two sons eventually took wives among the Moabite women, named Orpah and Ruth, even though the Israelites were commanded not to marry among pagan nations surrounding them. Just a few years previously, such a situation would have been unimaginable for Elimelech and his family. Now it was standard practice which produced inevitable tension between Naomi and her wayward husband.

There is no home as unhappy as a home divided about the things of God. As they began to settle materially, a deep religious issue remained outstanding.

"Do you realise we haven't been to worship God in weeks, Elimelech?"

"Don't panic, Naomi, give it time, it's hard to find the right spiritual environment when you move to a new place. It's all about settling in at this stage."

"Pardon me for saying, but since we arrived here, some people appear to have settled in Moab very well."

"What's that supposed to mean?"

"You know very well what it means, Elimelech. You don't pray anymore and all you do these days is work. When was the last time you mentioned God? I hardly recognise my husband; it's as though you've become the very thing you used to oppose."

"Can't you understand, Naomi, we're in Moab now? Things will never be the same as Israel. We have a new life here, forget the past and enjoy the future. The future belongs to Moab!"

"Forget the past? Forget the past; the future belongs to Moab? Just listen to you. Have we lived our whole lives in Israel for nothing? We're only here, and already you sound like the Moabites. Before we came to Moab, did you ever consider where we would worship, socialise, and pray?"

"We'll cross that bridge in time, Naomi. Let's get our material situation sorted out first."

"The Law of Moses is our priority, Elimelech."

Naomi sighed heavily and went outside. Frightened and tearful, she gazed at the night sky, the stars shining down on her weather-beaten and by now weary face.

What had they done?

Is it possible that this once highly respected and blessed family in Israel had reached such a "spiritually bankrupt" point in their lives?

Naomi suddenly became conscious of how she wasn't only in danger of losing their religious culture, but also her husband as she once knew him. Looking up to the heavens, she cried out desperately to her Creator from the depths of her soul: Oh God, this situation is beyond me. Only you can soften and change the heart of my dear husband. Please speak to him Lord, before it's too late.

But it was already too far too late.

Elimelech had broken free from the bondage of his religious ritual and the Law of Moses. Gone were the extended dutiful gatherings in Bethlehem.

No more pretending by Elimelech. For the first time in years, he could do as he pleased. He was "free as a bird" and "ready to fly."

Elimelech had previously been under constraints in his own life! He was tired trying to keep a standard he knew was impossible and equally exhausted playing church! Ritualism can make any religion feel mundane, while legalism liberates no one.

So, in his eyes, moving to Moab was a masterstroke in terms of managing the situation and birthing a new career. After they'd arrived, one of the first things he did was to dispense with any religious attire, replacing it with clothing more representative of the Moabite culture.

He no longer wanted to be known as "an Israelite."

Israel?

Bethlehem?

The Law of Moses?

That was well behind him now. For him, it was a case of all things new and all things possible.

Far off fields appeared green as he set out on his new exciting adventure.

In time, Elimelech adjusted to the ways of the Moabites, just like the many other Israelites who'd moved there to escape the famine and were now living and successfully integrating into that community.

Initially, Elimelech found the freedom he'd long since craved.

The usual boundaries associated with the Law of Moses had disappeared. There was no religious accountability and nothing to restrain his rebellious character. Answerable to no one, he began to enjoy his lack of restrictions, thus widening the gap between himself and his devout wife. Even her obvious distress and her best protestations had failed to touch the heart of Elimelech leaving her anxious and concerned. She'd even tried a softer approach but to no avail!

Moab was his decision and his alone.

To be pushed into a situation, therefore, where Naomi was forced to live somewhere other than her much-loved homeland cannot be taken lightly. What an ordeal for this staunch Jewish woman.

Remember, she was a Hebrew, robustly fond of the customs of her religion. A regular worshipper in Bethlehem, and a woman of prayer, Naomi was much loved and useful, an encourager, and a highly popular woman of great faith and consistency.

An 'all or nothing' person, when Naomi signed up for something, she was there rain, hail or shine; there was no 'halfway house' or 'supermarket faith.'

On the contrary, Naomi was a member of one temple, one God, and one faith. She would have prayed in the morning, again at lunchtime, and in the evening, not in the ritualistic manner some experience, but because her heart desired the presence of God.

She would regularly tell her husband Elimelech: "God has given me a zeal for His house. I'm not here because I have to be, I'm here because I want to be."

You see, Naomi believed in a relationship, not a religion. Naomi knew the true and living God.

Consider the pain therefore that this woman endured having been forced to live in a pagan land like Moab where prayer and worship to Jehovah didn't exist, where people attended church for what they could get rather than what they could give?

Suddenly Naomi found herself stuck in the mud with turkeys when she should have been soaring with eagles?

Naomi had no desire to leave Israel, but agreed to, not because she was tired of scarcity, instead she was a genuinely submissive and obedient wife to her husband, as was the culture in those days. But having now left Bethlehem, both she and her husband had waived any right to the usual freedom of worship they once enjoyed.

Often we don't appreciate how great privilege being free to worship the true and living God is until we're required to reside in a place that not only prohibits such veneration but punishes people severely for their devotion to God.

Things were not a great deal different in Elimelech and Naomi's day. When it came to religion and God, Moab was the polar opposite of Israel, so it's more than likely Naomi, and her family would have experienced opposition even though the family's move to Moab initially proved successful and welcoming. We know this because they managed to live for some years without notable incident, but immense tragedy still lay in wait for all of them — and how? Tragedy always strikes when we least expect.

It was a hot, sticky day when Naomi's nightmare first began. Elimelech and the boys had gone to work, and like most days she remained at home, cooling in the shade. Like many tragic and unforeseen incidents, there was absolutely no warning. Pottering about, and singing, Naomi's soul was at rest until the cries of neighbours caught her attention with horrifying news.

"What is it, what is it?" she exclaimed.

"Can we sit down, Naomi?"

"Why, what's the matter?"

"There's been a terrible accident."

"What sort of accident?"

Straight away Naomi's heart sank. She knew it was Elimelech, but didn't want to believe it. From the time they'd set foot in Moab, she was repeatedly troubled about how something tragic might occur, something awful, and now it had happened. Like Job, the thing she most feared had come upon her.

"Is it Elimelech? Please, tell me he is okay?"

"Oh, my dear Naomi, we're so sorry; he slipped

and fell and banged his head, and when we heard, we ran to the scene, but found him barely awake and bleeding badly."

Naomi sprinted to the scene with Ruth at her side and found Elimelech almost at death's door. They told him not to speak and to lie still, but it was obvious he wanted to say something. He knew right then he would die and his last words needed to be words of repentance, if not to his God, then at least to his loyal and devoted wife. She, of all people, didn't deserve what was about to happen.

"If it's any consolation, Naomi, I'm sorry for forcing you to leave your people and culture. I want you to know how much I love you and I ask your forgiveness for this. I was just concerned for you and the boys, for all of us, and wanted a better life."

"It's all right, Elimelech, truly it is, my dear. Just be still, help is on the way. You need all of your strength now. We can worry about those things later."

But later wouldn't come and despite Naomi's words of comfort it was too late. Elimelech lay conscious for a short time, he even spoke again briefly, but in the end death took him.

Realising her husband had passed away, Naomi let out a scream that would have been heard back in Israel. In that moment her soul became crushed. No amount of hugs from her well-meaning neighbours could console her and nothing could have prepared her for such misfortune.

"No..., please, please no! Not my Elimelech! Oh, dear Lord, why?"

Having collapsed, weeping uncontrollably, and with her head bowed, the tears rolled from Naomi's beautiful eyes. Not just the tears of a woman who had lost her husband; there was a deeper, more complicated reason behind her outpouring of grief. It was those final words of her husband. They would follow her for the rest of her life, words of comfort, yet words of regret and the thought of what might have been.

Naomi had loved her devoted but impetuous husband. He was her world. She believed he was a good man who'd just lost his way. There was a kindness deep down inside this man that only Naomi had truly understood and been party to. Elimelech would have given a stranger his bed and the shirt off his back.

She'd always known that it was a risk to leave Israel, but now here she was picking up the pieces of an appalling decision. Reflecting on how they'd been in Moab for well over a decade; it suddenly occurred to her how she couldn't remember a single day of joy, or visualise a time when she felt at peace and experienced genuine prosperity in their new country. Instead, death and sorrow had visited her, leaving her in the unimaginable position of being stranded and widowed in a foreign land.

The ungodly Moabites delighted in mocking her seemingly unrewarded faith? They worshipped false gods and became enemies of Israel, even calling on Balaam to curse God's people. Upon hearing of Naomi's misfortune, it wasn't long before the locals began to rub their hands with glee in the local market place.

"Poor Naomi, she'd have been better off staying in Israel."

"So young to be a widow and to think she prays every day."

"Prays? Who to? If it's her God, he doesn't appear to be listening."

"Well, what else might she have expected? She hasn't embraced our gods and that move from Israel was always an accident waiting to happen."

Meanwhile, the devastated Naomi continued to cling on to some remaining hope in life. After all, her two sons were still alive, and that's where she now needed to concentrate all of her energy. Managing to cope with Elimelech's passing for some years afterwards, she did just that, pouring herself into the lives of her sons and their wives Ruth and Orpah, in an attempt to block out the immense loss that was Elimelech. It was a tactic which worked for some time until once again, death returned in merciless fashion; this time robbing her of not one, but both of her sons Mahlon and Chilion, their names a disturbing prophecy of their lives meaning "sickly" and "wasting."

Chilion died suddenly from disease having suffered from bad health most of his life. Naomi had always sensed he might not live too long, so wasn't surprised at his passing, but the death of her other son, Mahlon proved the final straw.

It seemed to kill any strength she had left. It was a death like Elimelech's, unexpected and unwelcome. The straw which broke the camel's back!

Mahlon suffered heat stroke from working tirelessly as the sole provider left in the family. Repeatedly encouraged to slow down and rest, he ignored the advice of his mother and wife Ruth and paid the price for it.

He was the man of the house and couldn't stop himself. He believed he had a duty and responsibility to help provide for his family. Unlike his father and Chilion, however, Mahlon died a slow, cruel death, this despite Naomi's strong faith for his healing. His deeply spiritual mother had prayed many times for God to ease her son's pain and truly believed God would answer those prayers. Indeed right to the end, she had held to the "promises of God" and continued to believe that all things were possible. She'd quoted scripture to her son and herself and reminded him that God does miracles. Ruth, too, was in anguish about her husband's state of health but Naomi constantly told her not to worry.

"You'll see Ruth, God will heal the surviving man in our lives," Naomi would say to Ruth.

Mahlon was their life, but both of them felt powerless to help him. They lost count of the nights when they would attend his bedside to try and aid his recovery. Losing Mahlon would leave them bereft and with no male providers, an insulting and unbearable prospect. It wasn't just grief and a lack of finance that was at stake. If Mahlon died, too, Naomi would have to endure terrible stigma; it was considered a blessing from God to have a large family, but to be a widow with no child was to be known even by the Jews as among the lowest and most afflicted of classes. Struggling for acceptance in a foreign land, she would now face rejection from her own people.

Even worse, the Jews considered such people to be under a curse due to some sin in their family. They believed that God had commanded them to be fruitful and multiply something expected of every Jewish family.

Nevertheless, all she and Ruth could do was watch and cry as, day after day, Mahlon deteriorated. In his final hours, Naomi's remaining son just lay there and stared unable to help himself. His fate was in the hands of God and God alone, and Naomi knew it. The clock was ticking and ticking fast.

Her sorrow over the death of her husband followed by the loss of Chilion had already consumed her for many years and months.

She didn't need this.

She didn't deserve it.

She couldn't take one more blow.

It didn't seem fair!

It was bad enough losing Elimelech and Chilion, but surely not Mahlon also!

Surely, surely not him too!

What did God expect of her?

She'd believed God could and would heal her remaining son, yet unimaginably, before her very eyes, it didn't happen, and, like his father and brother before him, poor Mahlon slipped into eternity leaving Naomi alone.

What do we do when the thing we pray and believe for are no longer possible?

What do we do when the cruellest and most unexpected of events transpire?

How do we react when all hope appears to have disappeared and we didn't receive the outcome we believed for?

Do we continue to trust God in such awful conditions or abandon our faith?

Here's something to consider! It can take months, even years to discover that, in such tragic circumstances, God is still there, still at work, and God can bring good out of the kind of misfortune and pain the like of which Naomi was experiencing.

Of course, Naomi wasn't the only one hurting. Ruth had responded to Mahlon's tragic death in the same way her mother-in-law had done when Elimelech had passed away and similar to Orpah when Chilion also died.

Grief-stricken and filled with sorrow, Naomi, Ruth, and Orpah were now left in a house of mourning beyond most people's comprehension. Three women undergoing enormous heartache, the sadness was overwhelming and the sense of pain inconceivable.

Reverberating daily in Naomi's ears, the words of her two sons before they died were all she could hear: "We should never have come to Moab. Father should have kept us in Bethlehem. This place is a cursed mother."

Who could have argued?

Not Naomi.

Not Ruth.

Not Orpah.

Elimelech's untimely death and the passing of Naomi's two precious sons created considerable devastation and provoked some profoundly troubling and soul-searching questions for the grieving and godly Naomi.

Did we step out of God's will when we chose to leave Israel?

Was Elimelech wrong to move to Moab, even if it was to avoid the famine?

Could I have done more to stop Elimelech leaving our homeland?

Is God punishing us for some sin and worse might he also have abandoned us as well?

The total size of the tragedy she'd encountered certainly suggested something was severely wrong and when this happens disturbing questions like the ones Naomi had often follow. This lady had lost everything dear to her, only gaining in return the lesson that while things may look attractive elsewhere, they are not necessarily any better.

Far off fields are not always greener!

The family's calamitous move from the famine-ravished state of Israel had produced an incredible and extraordinary situation for Naomi and her two foreign daughters-in-law. Bereavement and widowhood cruelly tossed her grandest ambitions into the gutter.

Elimelech's decision to leave Israel wasn't just reckless; it was life changing — a truth, Naomi, Ruth, and Orpah had discovered only too well — and sadly to their severe cost.

Three

Unbearable

"Then Mahlon and Chilion died, and Naomi was left without her two sons." (Ruth 1:3)

Naomi awakened reluctantly, the hunger pains pushing her out of bed in a remote part of Moab. God had blessed her with another day, but it felt like a curse. The home was cramped and cluttered; unrecognisable compared to what she'd left behind in Israel many years before — a house adorned with fancy rugs, sophisticated tables, and linen curtains.

Disorientated, she stumbled and staggered past an old wooden bench, with an empty plate and spoon on it, a horrible reminder of yesterday's lack of provision. The sun wasn't entirely up, but it was already hot and sticky, and her throat was parched.

She watched the natives going about their business on the busy streets outside her humble home. The roads would quickly fill, thronged with people trying to make a living. By contrast, Naomi's only wish at this stage was to survive. Buried in another country and separated from her kinsfolk, she wondered if she would ever see them again; if she would ever laugh, hope and live again. The enormity of the situation had suddenly hit home. She felt sick to the pit of her stomach and horrified by the costs of decisions which were too late to alter; decisions which threatened to end her life and had hampered her utmost dreams.

"Oh God, have mercy on me," cried Naomi. "How on earth has it come to this?"

Left in the impossible position of having to care for her two daughters-in-law, Naomi's fears were more than justified. Alone and in a strange land, how indeed would she provide, not only for herself but the two girls?

Things were no better in Moab than in Israel all those years ago when famine had forced them out. The men in her life gone, the crops had perished too following another famine in Moab. Nothing grew there anymore, and, as far as Naomi was concerned, nothing would grow there again.

Opening the door Naomi could see the road that led from Moab to Judah from the hillside near her home, because of the stunning view of the mountains where they had initially settled, but nothing in her life made sense anymore. Her future was uncertain. To even consider tomorrow sent shivers down her spine.

"Give us this day our daily bread" became her only prayer.

This God-fearing woman's mind and heart were in abject turmoil. With no income, hardly clothed and living on sympathy, it wasn't the life Naomi was used to in Israel or had even dreamed during her youth. Back then she had such high hopes for herself and her family. Not in an arrogant way, more a natural desire to succeed in life. She wanted her family, friends, and brethren to be proud of her and had imagined such a scene on countless occasions.

Like most young girls she believed she would grow into a princess and marry a prince; instead, her story had become a nightmare. Everything lay in tatters. She hadn't truly appreciated the joyous times until they were replaced by devastation.

Life, as it often does, had changed in an instant.

A servant of God, she appeared to have been visited by the prince of darkness, death, and destruction.

Growing up, Naomi would have been encouraged to believe in a merciful and loving God, one who can meet all of our needs. She had high expectations for herself having been taught the blessings of God from an early age, but life had thrown her an unexpected curve ball leaving her abandoned. No one could blame her for questioning her faith, decisions, and even her very existence! Here was lady experiencing the aftermath of a tragedy uncommon to most people. To lose a husband is bad enough; to watch her sons die, too, was cruel beyond words. No parent expects to outlive their children and see them buried or be left to have to provide for foreign relatives in a strange land.

Could it get any worse?

Struggling with immense grief and loss, she still had three mouths to feed. She had bills and responsibilities, but from where would the source come? Who would offer a Hebrew widow like Naomi a job in Moab, even if she was fit for work? Mentally and physically, how would she have functioned following such a series of blows?

Losing a loved one, a spouse or a child is a devastating occurrence for anyone, and the trauma associated with such events is considerable, but the triple tragedy of losing her husband and two sons? Like a tsunami tearing through a city, the aftermath of these fierce interruptions is life-altering.

It can take substantial time to recover from such shattering experiences; nevertheless, Naomi would learn that when God is present healing and spiritual growth is still possible, even at the most traumatic and unlikely time. She would discover how it's still possible to develop in horrible places and become stronger.

The name Naomi means "pleasant" or "my joy," yet things were far from pleasant and joyful in Moab at this terrifying stage of her life.

On the contrary, every day was drudgery; every hour uncertain. Previously Naomi had been a delightful, pleasing and eye-catching woman until death and destruction caused her to lose both her swagger and self-esteem.

And, oh how she could swagger!

When Naomi hit the streets, heads turned. Once the envy of every woman due to her inner beauty and the object of every man, for her stunning outward complexion, she became a shadow of her former self, a recluse living in fear and self-condemnation. Even her dazzling beauty spot which decorated her face had lost its glow. People everywhere, especially Elimelech, commented on that cute little beauty spot. He had adored it, yet along with the decline of her dreams, the beauty spot too had faded from view.

Shame and guilt had visited her doorstep in an unthinkable manner. This once proud and confident Israelite had locked herself away, no longer socialising and reaching out to people in the way she'd once done. Having suffered such a horrendous tragedy, who could blame her? She was beyond overwhelmed. Her world had ended, and she never wanted to go out again.

Of course, the situation had left her exactly where the enemy of her soul wanted her — isolated and out of service, ineffective, fearful of the future and focusing on the past.

Her isolation became a safe place, a spot where she would never get hurt again when, separation is the most dangerous place a child of God like Naomi can be.

Here she became easy prey for the voice of discouragement. She'd accepted the bait to remove herself from public life, and so the battle for her mind began, spiritual warfare of a magnitude she'd never encountered before. Now the devil would have a field-day with righteous Naomi.

In Luke chapter four we read of how the same devil tried to destroy Jesus in the very same way over a forty-day period, a destructive dialogue which took place in isolation in the wilderness. Fortunately, the Bible records how Jesus resisted him and even returned from this trying period of remoteness in "the power of the spirit."

Similarly, it was during her time of seclusion that Naomi became easy prey for the voice of the accuser — the enemy of her soul.

"Look at you, how could you be a child of God? No children and no provision, you're a woman cursed, and you will never be anything again."

"Stop it, stop it, I don't want to hear it," yelled Naomi, but relentlessly her adversary persisted.

"It's over for you, do you hear me, over! All of your former friends are doing well and look at the state of you? How can you pray, witness or worship again? Who will take you seriously? Who would even listen to someone like you? Your family must be ashamed of you and what must they think of your so-called God now? No husband, no children, and no future."

She found it hard to argue. Through choice, she'd shut herself away with only this malicious and pitiless voice of negativity for company.

All Naomi could see was an unfulfilled life, broken dreams and a hopeless future. Even the ungodly Moabites appeared more blessed than she was.

How could this be?

And, so, for the first time in her spiritual life, huge doubts began to emerge — why, for example, had they ever set foot in such a place?

Why is all of this happening to her?

"Why me, Lord, why, why, why?"

Despite Elimelech's former optimism, Naomi didn't know who she was anymore or even where she was. With regard to who would provide for her two daughters-in-law, she had another pressing issue. She was terrified to mention the subject to them; to anyone. She'd tried to keep her situation a secret, but in time the whole world knew the truth — Naomi was in trouble!

What do you do when you have a problem so big you can no longer keep it a secret?

What do you do when it leaks out the door, and everyone gets to hear about it?

For a while, you manage to cover it up, but eventually, it becomes public news, clear to all and sundry that you're in difficulty and that you require urgent assistance, even a miracle!

The Moabites noticed and relished this downward trend in Naomi's life and immediately rejoiced at the misfortune of the holy lady from Israel.

"Look at her and her household. Coming here to evangelise and try and tell us how to live and she can't even run her own house."

"Cheek of her! She deserves all she gets. She was always too prim and proper for my liking. Miss Goody Two Shoes, she was forever moralising to her husband and obsessed with the worship of that god of hers."

"Well, let's see how big her so-called god is now! Will he come through for her or will we get the satisfaction of watching her grovel and then die in the dust like her husband and sons?"

With no one to support her, Naomi knew from here on she would have to rely on the generosity of strangers, even people who had no time for her. So perhaps the Moabites had a point?

Here was a child of God begging bread!

A woman destined for greatness living like a pauper! An Israelite, no less, from a former well to do family, someone who once had influence and position, a call on their life and a purpose, someone revered, admired and respected, wondering where the next meal was coming!

A child of the King broke, busted and disgusted!

The words of Psalm 37 say; *"I have been young, and now I am old, yet I have never seen the righteous forsaken or their children begging bread."* (Psalm 37: 5)

This text is often preached erroneously in our modern day to suggest we only have the favour of God when there is provision available, something which is to the detriment of many believers going through hard times.

God is as much with us when we have nothing as He is when we have abundance and sometimes even more so!

The Apostle Paul wrote; *"I have learned, in whatsoever state I am, therewith to be content. I know both how to be abased, and I know how to abound; everywhere and in all things I am instructed both to be full and to be hungry, both to abound and to suffer need."* (Philippians 4:11-12)

Notwithstanding the people of Moab and the watching Israelites probably still wondered why there was a lack of bread on the great Naomi's table, why had someone so highly favoured become destitute?

Why had God seemingly abandoned her?

Such negative questions always emerge from those who fail to grasp the loving and restorative nature of God or the reality of this life.

It was approaching Christmas and the children were excited. Sharon (not her real name) had just dropped her two boys off at school and was heading home to put up their Christmas tree. There was a huge traffic jam caused by an apparent accident. Sharon became frustrated because she was looking forward to erecting the tree and wrapping presents for her two boys and "special husband" who had left for work earlier that morning. Then word began to filter through that a man had been fatally injured in a car resembling her husband's and was lying on the ground just a few hundred yards away. Sharon's heart stopped. She didn't want to believe it, but already a sinking feeling had come over her.

What if it is her husband?

Surely not!

She couldn't bear to wait any longer and decided to do the unthinkable by getting out of her car and rushing to the scene. At first, police wouldn't allow her through, but when she recognised her husband's car and explained why she was concerned, and it was confirmed that her husband was indeed dead at the scene, Sharon was finally allowed through the cordon where she fell grief stricken at the feet of her husband.

How would she tell the boys?

How would she cope in general?

What about Christmas and the one after and the one after that?

How could she face life at all from there on?

Thankfully Sharon had a close circle of family and friends and received incredible support from all of them, but once the funeral passed and the cards stopped and the house calls ceased too, she knew she was left to pick up the pieces and try and carry on with life.

Her children were, of course, equally devastated by the loss of their father, and rebelled for some time afterwards. It was a horrendous time, a life-changing situation which produced incredible stress levels for them all. Then, one evening, while sitting at home Sharon picked up a book. For months she'd stopped reading, even the reading of the Bible because her heart was too broken. She suddenly realised she'd stopped praying also, but God is merciful and He more than anyone understood the pain she had endured. The writer of Hebrews records how Christ is *"touched with the feelings of our infirmities."* (Hebrews 4:15)

He knows our needs and our struggles and identifies with us at times of overwhelming grief.

The book Sharon had reached for was a story of a woman who had lost everything, but later in life enjoyed the goodness and grace of God in ways she could never have imagined. It is true that sometimes dreadful things happen to ordinary people, yet God's grace is always there, and God's restoring power is ever present. Then Sharon saw the words "Incidents do happen, and God understands when we have questions."

For the first time in ages, Sharon revived, determined to turn things around. Suddenly she realised she hadn't brought anything on herself. It was one of those awful life moments which some people have to endure, yet God still had tremendous plans for her life. In the midst of chaos, grief and many questions, His grace was still available for her.

Suffering is not necessarily a sign that God has removed His grace from us. There's nothing we can do to earn God's grace or blessing. It is a gift from Him because of the finished work of Jesus on the cross at Calvary. Jesus was the only perfect man who ever lived, and yet they crucified Him at the cross. He constantly did the right thing but was still rejected by His people at Nazareth and then ultimately hung upon a cross.

Suffering or hardship doesn't always denote consequences of sin. It is true we can reap what we sow, but not always and sometimes suffering is just part of identifying with the suffering Christ. The apostle Paul, who had his share of persecution and trials, highlighted the great cost in following God stating; *"That I may know him, and the power of his resurrection, and the fellowship of his sufferings, Being made conformable unto his death."* (Philippians 3:10)

The Bible says; *"Through many tribulations we must enter the kingdom of God"* (Acts 14:22). We must be conscious of the fact that while here on earth, the New Jerusalem of no tears and no pain, of no mourning and no death, hasn't arrived yet. (Revelation 21)

Life is about joy and pain, hardship and blessing; life is about lessons and seasons which will benefit the people coming behind us. Naomi was not an exception to this rule no matter how unpleasant it felt. She had honoured God and had lived a godly life, she'd been more faithful than her husband, but she was now enduring the most unthinkable of seasons and circumstances. She had no family in Moab and no one else to come to her aid, a desperate situation for anyone, let alone a poor widow.

The Christian life is often painted as a "bed of roses" — a life without complications and setbacks — yet from Genesis to Revelation we read of many biblical giants, great servants of God like Naomi who went through severe testing, trials and persecutions. In all probability, these people were more faithful to God than you and I, yet many of them still struggled to survive and endured some shocking trials. The world viewed them as failures, but in the eyes of God and Heaven, they were successful.

While others took no risks and protected their interests, these faithful servants of God stepped out in faith in response to the leading of the Lord and paid a heavy price.

They refused the accolades of this present world, preferring instead the crown of life in Heaven. The book of Hebrews mentions these individuals creating an image of success that the world we live in and many in the Church today fail to grasp.

Bible greats such as Abel, Abraham, Jacob, Joseph, Moses, Rahab, Gideon, Barak, Samson, Jephthah, David, Samuel, and many other prophets fall into the following category.

"Who through faith, conquered kingdoms, stopped the mouths of lions, quenched the power of fire, escaped the edge of the sword, were made strong out of weakness, became mighty in war, put foreign armies to flight. Women received back their dead by resurrection. Some were tortured, refusing to accept release so that they might rise again to a better life. Others suffered mocking and flogging and even chains and imprisonment. They were stoned, they were sawn in two, and they were killed with the sword. They went about in skins of

sheep and goats, destitute, afflicted, and mistreated – of whom the world was not worthy – wandering about in deserts and mountains and dens and caves of the earth."
(Hebrews 1:32-38)

How did these people keep serving God in such barbaric conditions? By the grace of God and genuine faith. The apostle Paul also wrote, *"We are afflicted in every way, but not crushed; perplexed but not driven to despair; persecuted, but not destroyed."* (2 Corinthians 4:8-9)

Paul lists several forms of suffering — mental, physical emotional, and spiritual. When suffering and unbearable pain occurs like this, living a life of a recluse is a bad idea because as Naomi later discovered there is much comfort to be found in our relationships with others. Herein the church can play a significant part in helping restore and revive those who are broken and under spiritual attack. No situation is too drastic to bring to God.

In one of the parables of Jesus he tells how the master told the servant of his house to; *"go out quickly into the lanes of streets of the city and bring in the poor, crippled, blind and lame."* (Luke 4:21 ESV)

Jesus was saying: The church is a hospital for sick people.

When a fellow believer is hurting, the church applies the bandages, when they are disappointed and discouraged, the church encourages and when they are desperately in need the church draws alongside and helps. At least, that's what's supposed to take place. What happens if the church fails in its duty of care and shamefully neglects their wounded as is the case all too frequently? What transpires if others lack compassion and leave troubled souls to suffer alone?

Then God promises to be with us regardless of which valley we are in. Isaiah wrote; *"When you pass through the* waters, I will be with you and when you pass through the rivers, they will not sweep over you. When you walk through the fire you will not be burned; the flames will not set you ablaze." (Isaiah 43:2)

Contrary to some viewpoints today, when it comes to following and serving God, there's a cost. Coming to know Christ and embracing Christianity is not the easy route it's often presented as. Jesus said; "Whoever does not take up his cross and follow me cannot be my disciple." (Luke 14:27)

Like all of the biblical heroes who went through trials and extensive suffering, Naomi is a victim in this story, but the point to highlight is this — eventually, she would become a victor! She'd honoured God and had lived a devout life but was still made to endure the most unbearable of seasons and circumstances before reaching her final destination.

In the words of Peter; "And the God of all grace, who called you to his eternal glory in Christ, after you have suffered a little while, will himself restore you and make you strong, firm and steadfast." (1 Peter 5:10)

She was left without family in Moab, no one else to come to her aid, a desperate situation for anyone, let alone a single woman.

Like Job, Naomi lost her nearest and dearest and faced a bleak future. The sense of loneliness greatly exacerbated the loss she now felt as she found herself detached from her closest friends and acquaintances.

Unlike today, neither could she avail of any support mechanism within society in Moab designed to protect foreign widows or provide for them. She and her foreign daughters would just have to learn to battle on.

As she stared at the ground in her empty home in Moab, the crushing reality of what had taken place in her life finally began to sink in. Picture three anxious widows with no income and no providers!

No matter how spiritual we think we are, or how robust we've proved previously, when events turn against us in such an unruly way, the best of God's people question themselves — and sometimes God, too and when this occurs, there's always someone else observing it. That someone is frequently ready to view just how much faith people who say they believe in God truly have. In this case, it was, of course, the Moabites and Naomi's adopted daughters, Ruth and Orpah. They, in particular, were all too aware of Naomi's predicament but had remained silent throughout. They'd always been impressed with their mother-in-law and her remarkable faith, but following the separate tragedies, a searching question remained unanswered for both — an issue they hadn't been required to face previously - how would Naomi now react to such immense personal misfortune?

Would she continue to remain faithful to her God or, in the words of Job's wife, would she *"curse God and die?"* (Job 2:9)

Would she stay strong or capitulate?

Would she blame God indefinitely, or accept life's cruellest turns?

This appalling disaster was a bridge too far for anyone, let alone her?

Surely no one, not even sweet, charming and determined Naomi, could make it back from here?

Four

Why is this happening to me?

"In the world, you will have persecution, but be of good cheer for I have overcome the world."
(John 16:33)

The sun rose, bringing yet another day of recriminations and regret. Naomi had experienced inconceivable situations which were not of her making. Some people create their own storms and then get upset when it rains, but not Naomi.

So, with face down on the floor; she began to pray, not a common prayer like the others; this time a more frantic cry for help from the depths of her heart from someone not sure if they could take another step in life.

"I want to make it and recover from this curse upon my life, but you are going to have to strengthen me, Lord. I am so weak and beyond help other than your help. Please visit us with your kindness and mercy for I know you are a merciful God," she cried.

Suddenly she noticed her two daughters in law chatting outside of the house.

Hadn't they been through grief also?

Didn't they deserve to be protected?

Wouldn't they require consolation and encouragement?

And so, for the first time in ages, it dawned on Naomi how she'd been looking inwardly, not outwardly. She'd become obsessed with her own problems and immersed in self-pity. Had she drifted so far from the compassion which once came naturally to her? Had she become so far removed from others, especially the needs of the girls? Naomi knew she had little in common with either Ruth or Orpah spiritually, but they were her family, and she loved them like her own. She had tried continuously to witness to them about her faith in God, but the greatest witness she could demonstrate was a faith and a compassion which functioned no matter what life had dealt her. Besides, Ruth and Orpah were all she had left.

As they both walked and chatted outside, Naomi's eyes filled with tears and her heart swelled with sympathy for them.

Look at them? God bless them both, they must wonder what on earth is going on. If I can't understand things and I have God in my life, how confused they must be. Poor little souls! They look so bereft, bruised and bereaved. What have I been doing all these months focusing on me and my problems? I haven't been there for them the way I should have been. After all, my questions are their questions also.

Then it struck Naomi how all of them did have something in common. Naomi and the two girls were now widows. It was not the point to pull away from her daughters-in-law, but a time to draw closer to them. She knew deep in her heart that nothing united people like collective grief, yet how does one reach out and help others with a broken heart and crushed spirit?

Please, Lord, we are all so hungry, hurt and disappointed, it's as though we have nothing left to give, but we will not give up. Heal our Land, Lord; I know you can heal our land. Heal me, too, Lord, for I feel so damaged and confused.

That powerful prayer was evidence of Naomi's returning faith, a faith battered and bruised yes, but a faith about to be resurrected. For months this broken woman had sat in a gloomy state, reminiscing about Israel, dreaming of better days and happier times. Trapped in a dark corner of the room she found solace embracing an era where she once had everything — a good husband, two sons, and a family anticipating an exciting future. Now, following the deaths of her husband and sons, how could there be any existence without Elimelech and the boys? Where was the sense in it all? It seemed so unfair that in that sticky, humid environment, all she had left were memories. No wonder she held on to them with all that she had, especially her recollections of better days in Bethlehem. Such reminiscing was more than a crutch; it sustained her and helped keep her alive, but to continue in this state would prove counterproductive because no one can move forward while looking back.

Thriving?

She was barely surviving, and time waits for no one. We are all subject to a fast ticking clock.

Change continues at a relentless pace and has no respect for persons or situations.

The longer she sat and stared into space, the more the world around her, oblivious to her circumstances, raced on.

In her grief, she wondered how others could be so joyful and insensitive when going through such immense suffering. Did they not recognise her misery and pain? Why were they so thoughtless and disrespectful?

The reality is, when we are in a season of mourning, loss, and grief, it's hard for others to understand the depth of our hurt truly. While many are just getting on with their lives, grief paralyses and puts other people's lives on hold. Naomi was no exception.

At such times it's important to dream of better days and more affluent, happier times, but focusing on the past obstructs true peace.

In a deep depression, it was only a matter of time before Naomi became fixated on her spectacular demise.

What had caused this phenomenal fall from grace?

Why had she ended up on skid row?

Considered so loving, kind and gracious, how come Naomi met with such appalling misfortune?

The questions kept coming, but the answers failed to show up.

"If only I could go back in time and relive that period of my life again."

There was a genuine level of frustration residing inside her. She was angry with herself having obeyed God, and her husband, before falling on hard times. Now Naomi longed to return to the point when it was easy to smile, and her heart didn't feel like it might break. She recalled her family and friends, people she loved and people who were precious to her. Naomi visited every microscopic detail about them. She missed their hugs and kisses and well wishes every day and must have posed the question why so many times.

Why did Naomi feel so guilty and personally responsible for their mess?

Why had this happened to her and her family?

Why has a loving and caring God allowed this to happen in the first place? Notably, nowhere in this story does Naomi mention anything about being punished by God for sin, but she still asked why such a tragedy had happened?

Don't pretend you've never been there. Why is a question millions of people, including Christians ask every day? The question "why?" is perfectly normal, and even rang out in the darkest hour of the New Testament when the Lord Jesus cried out; *My God, my God why have you forsaken me.* (Matthew 27:46)

With so much suffering in the world we could even add: Why does God allow such evil and sorrow to persist in the world?

Why are innocent people, many of whom are just going about their business, killed by terrorists? Why are there so many natural disasters, illnesses, abuse, crime, and death? Why is there an increase in betrayal, sorrow, injuries, disappointment, and heartache? Asking why is a natural question about all of these things, and yet the "why question" is nothing new.

Thousands of years ago, Bible greats including Job and King David all asked God why. During the 20th century, the question why continued especially during two world wars, the Holocaust, the Troubles in Northern Ireland, the emergence of diseases such as Aids and Cancer and the spread of dreadful global famines, tsunamis and earthquakes.

This century sees us asking why again.

The Iraq War preceded the tragic events of 9/11 and, due to the rise of religious extremism; we are now experiencing famine and slaughter on the streets of many cities throughout the world today.

If God is so loving and in control, then why are these things taking place? It's a natural question to ask.

A survey was undertaken some years ago to try and uncover the number one question people would like to ask God if they got such an opportunity. Unsurprisingly the response was: "Why is there so much suffering in the world?"

You may say, I've never asked God why and I don't intend to. I trust God completely.

If that's the case, I'm impressed, but you might end up asking why if tragedy strikes your home or loved ones in the same way as Naomi experienced. When all is going well, it's easy not to ask why? What happens though when the sky falls in around you and your world comes crashing down? Asking why then becomes a reasonable course of action, not a betrayal of one's faith. It is perfectly reasonable to want to ask why we have to suffer so much.

We know that life produces love, joy, and peace; but it also includes suffering, sickness, and pain. While Christ proclaimed the good news of the gospel, He also stated; *"In the world, you will have persecution, but be of good cheer for I have overcome the world."* (John 16:33)

Christians are to expect trouble as well as triumph. Nevertheless, that doesn't answer our question of why difficulty is allowed in our lives or why all the above incidents mentioned in this chapter are permitted by a loving God.

Why, for example, are Christians being beheaded, killed and tortured by terrorists while God and man appear to sit back in silence? Why are people dying from homelessness, disease, and starvation? I don't believe anyone on this earth can fully answer such questions, especially this writer, but one day we will understand why.

For now, our finite minds cannot comprehend everything but there's comfort in knowing that in such times of trial, Jesus has promised to be with us and to deliver us and help us overcome any obstacles in our path. God is a good God, full of hope and restoration. From the Creation story in the garden of Eden in the opening book of the Bible, when humanity suffered from the fall until the story of Jesus shedding His blood on the cross for the forgiveness of sins and the restoration of humanity, God's purpose and plan is restorative. He is a constant restorer of His creation and He brings peace and goodwill toward all men.

That restorative nature was just as evident in Naomi's ungodly generation. Despite immense pain, Naomi, too, would later come to realise the mercy and goodness of God in her broken life. She may not have had all the answers at that cruel juncture, but deep down inside, Naomi somehow continued to cling to the belief that God loved her and had a plan for her life. Perhaps you are at the same crossroads as Naomi, and God wants you to trust Him for greater days ahead. He wishes to use your place of weakness and pain to bring you to a place of strength and joy.

In God's purpose for her life, Moab was a nation which brought Naomi immense distress, but while there she learned much about her Creator, herself and others. A bitter period in her life, her character came to be cleansed and enhanced by her enormous grief, yet somehow, she managed to retain the constant goodness that gave her personality an appealing charm. Like Joseph, Naomi eventually learned to live with the terrible, but not be crushed by it. Like Abraham, who returned from Egypt a better and more humble man, following his disastrous move from home, her constant honesty in assessing the reality of her circumstances was not a sign of unbelief, but of strength.

For Naomi, it was always essential to keep moving forward in faith, especially if she hoped to impact her two daughters in law, neither of whom had yet converted to the one true God — Jehovah.

Did she have issues?

Of course, she did!

She had many unanswered questions? She must have experienced severe doubts from time to time, too, but Naomi was a child of God, and her story was far from over.

Maybe you are exhausted by some situation?

Are you frustrated, even distraught? Is there a major "why question" in your life?

It's okay to vent our frustrations at God, so long as it doesn't become a habit and we reverence Him in our prayers. God wants us to become emotional and real with him. We are not robots or perfect people. The Bible says; *"This poor man cried and the Lord heard him and saved him out of all his troubles."* (Psalm 34:6)

Do you realise your story is not over yet either? God hasn't finished with you. He still has a grand plan to rescue and restore you even from the mouth of disaster and destruction, but how will you cope with seasons of loss before any gain?

How we handle disaster, tragedy, and disappointment, even significant hurts in our lives become crucial in our rehabilitation and in helping others to see how faith in God is not just from the teeth out. Naomi cried out to God and her prayers were heard.

Anyone can rejoice and worship when things are going well. It's easy to follow God when promotion arrives and popularity and position increases. It's simple to sing and clap and shout when all is well with the world, when everybody loves us, but how do we react when misfortune and adversity strikes?

As the daughters of Naomi watched on, filled with curiosity as to how their mother in law would respond to the unbelievable set-backs in her life, they would discover what Naomi had deep inside her heart — the spirit of the living God. They'd wondered was she merely a religious person, or a committed child of God?

Was she "good living for a living" or did she actually possess genuine faith?

It wasn't just Ruth and Orpah, but the whole of Moab was anticipating the answer. Huddled together in the corner, the girls watched and wondered too, whispering so as not to cause their mother in law any further anguish.

"Do you think Naomi is alright, Ruth?" asked Orpah.

"She seems tired and a bit spaced out. I'm worried about her. She sits in that chair and stares at the wall".

"Give her time, Ruth; she's grieving just like us. I mean, let's be fair, it must be so much worse for her having lost her entire family".

"We are her family now, Orpah and we must prove this and be strong for her."

"True, Ruth, but she needs to snap out of this and soon. She's got responsibilities and needs to face this.

How long is she going to sit there and do nothing?"

"Do you think Naomi is unaware of those responsibilities, Orpah? She is a woman in grief, give her a break."

"She's a woman who is losing her faith, Ruth."

"How can you say that? She's had one crisis after

another, and still, believes and prays which is more than I can say for you Orpah."

"I don't know what to believe anymore Ruth, but I know one thing; if that's how Naomi's God operates, I think I will stick with the gods in Moab."

The girls scampered back to their tasks, pretending all was normal, but Naomi already knew well what was going on. Beyond middle age, she had long since observed the respect her two daughters in law had for her; their faithfulness and kindness had touched her heart on numerous occasions. Naomi had always felt Ruth was more open to her Jewish roots and faith than Orpah, even though she loved them equally. She never made a distinction between them. Notwithstanding; left to care for not one, but two foreign daughters-in-law, wasn't Naomi's idea of a blessing.

It was, in fact, a severe insult, according to her culture, but God had other ideas. It wasn't the end for Naomi. Joy in the morning would replace her weeping for a night. She would eventually receive beauty for ashes and her best days were ahead, not behind.

Like Joseph, locked inside an Egyptian prison cell appearing finished and forgotten by men and God, little did he know he was still in the centre of God's will and about to move from the prison to the palace. Often our darkest hours are a sign of how close we are to our most celebrated days. Never underestimate God's power to restore even the most ruined areas of our lives. Naomi didn't. Joseph didn't and many other servants of God didn't.

Restoration is God's speciality!

Nevertheless, as she surveyed the wreckage of her own ruined life, it still must have felt like the end for poor Naomi.

As she sat there broken and beaten, she could only but cry out to her God because things seemed so unfair:

Why is this happening to me, God, why?

Is this it?

Is this as good as it gets?

Is there no hope of recovery?

And why are you so upset with me, God?

These are questions people ask when life doesn't turn out the way they expect, especially when affliction replaces blessing, poverty, affluence and when death savagely interrupts life. Do you realise it's possible to have great faith and still ask why?

In fact, it's normal to ask why and experience seasons of doubt and despair. Naomi had probably been told many times by insensitive and judgemental onlookers to "give herself a shake" and "move on," but remember, those insensitive advisors were not the victims of her harsh circumstances. They hadn't endured anywhere near the same pain level that this God-fearing lady had encountered, so how could they have empathised with the loss of her husband and later the passing of her two sons. It seemed cruel and counterproductive to tell Naomi, a woman in grief to "just get over it."

These insensitive individuals hadn't walked a metre let alone a mile in Naomi's shoes. Naomi may not have been prospering materially in Israel previously, but she and Elimelech were content and happy as a family. She was secure in her faith until that dreadful day when they all decided to leave home. And so further questions emerged about how she'd begged Elimelech not to go to Moab?

Hadn't she done the right thing?

Hadn't she sought God for Elimelech to change his heart and mind?

Hadn't she forgiven him and dreamed of seeing her two sons grow up to serve the Lord?

What more could she have done?

And, how was she rewarded for all this faith and persistence? Her children had become pagan in their ways and died prematurely like their father, leaving her abandoned and alone in a foreign land.

With a heart that was sore and confused, for the first time in her life, she not only questioned God but screamed out her frustration at Him in prayer. How could there be any purpose in such a personal mess? Then, finally her words expressed what had been pent up in her heart for so long, like a volcano erupting Naomi finally released what had been locked away for years.

Why have you done this to me, God, why? I tried to be obedient, I tried to talk Elimelech out of leaving, I decided to continue to bring the boys up learning your ways and teaching them your word, so why has all of this happened to me? I've done everything asked of me. I don't and never will understand it. Where are you right now, God? Where is your so-called provision? Oh, God, help me know. Why did you take my husband and my children, why did you leave me to die alone, why, why, why?

Breathless, Naomi hit the floor never wanting to get up again, but somehow, she managed the strength to rise and reach her worn-out chair.

As she clung to some old clothing of her late husband and children, all she could do was query her situation.

She didn't deserve this crisis, but Naomi would learn how life doesn't always give people what they deserve. In fact, life can be ferocious, and bad things do happen to good people and even to children of God. Everyone will reach a stage when it doesn't seem possible to carry on, but God will never settle for us on our face, His purpose is to see us on our feet.

Notwithstanding; Naomi's outburst of frustration was her way of making clear to God how she felt hard done by, even cheated in life. Her best efforts appeared to be met with failure and disappointment when she had seemingly done the right things leaving her feeling short-changed.

Maybe you feel similarly short-changed? Do you feel life has somehow cheated you? It's normal to feel hard done by when we've invested more than came back, something which sums up how Naomi must have felt in the wake of her tragic experiences in Moab.

She was always living with the feeling of regret which provoked her to ask God why?

Her situation became a massive test of her godly character. Would she continue to do the right thing when the wrong result occurred? When people are denied justice, it becomes a test of character and a sign of whether we truly love God or not.

However, just because she was robbed of justice didn't mean she was beyond survival ad success. The Old Testament Patriarch Job is one such example. Although he lost everything, his house, children and possessions, somehow, he still found the strength to say; *"Though he will slay me yet will I trust him."* (Job 13:15)

That same trust saw God restore unto Job three times what he had possessed previously.

Naomi couldn't see it then, but in time would come to realise something similar and precious about her God; He makes everything beautiful in His time.

She would find how life is repeatedly an unreasonable playing ground, but it's still possible to compete and continue. She knew the feeling of inequality having played by the rules and then discovered that the rules are not fair and, sometimes the rules don't matter.

The only course of action remaining was to make peace with this life upheaval, move on and trust her God, or continue to languish in self-pity and struggle indefinitely.

What other choice did she have? Courage does not always roar. Sometimes, it is the quiet voice at the end of the day saying, 'I will try again tomorrow.'

Naomi had arrived at this defining moment, a moment we all experience at some point in our lives — a moment of truth. To understand the 'why'; she would have to wait for 'when'.

Five

Who Told You to Stop Dreaming?

And Pharaoh said to Joseph, "I have dreamed a dream, and no one can interpret it. But I have heard it said of you that when you hear a dream, you can interpret it. "I cannot do it", Joseph replied to Pharaoh, "but God will give Pharaoh the answer he desires." (Genesis 41:14–16)

As nightfall approached, Naomi became delirious. Trapped in the small house in Moab they had occupied in exchange for luxury in Israel, she remained in a trance, yet God cared too much to leave her there. He would ultimately revive her spirit and restore her soul and, in a most familiar way — through the power of dreams! Do we realise how powerful dreams from God can be in helping us recover from the most horrendous experiences?

Like Joseph, who couldn't see the sky for many years, yet still emerged from the black hole of a prison cell, Naomi knew all about a dark, cold, empty dungeon where demoralisation and depression were rampant.

Joseph, of course, is the most renowned Bible character when it comes to dreams and visions.

His story is notable.

Joseph's gift was not only to dream but to interpret dreams and how the church could do with a Joseph again today?

In a world of so much confusion and subtlety, of little wisdom and no discernment, how we need a man like Joseph again!

So impressed was King Pharaoh with Joseph's ability to interpret dreams he said; *"Where can we find such a one as this, a man in whom the Spirit of God lives."* (Genesis 41:38)

Nevertheless, Joseph is also an outstanding example of how those same gifts are often hindered by the schemes, indifference and sometimes jealousy of man or through negative life incidents. The life of Joseph is proof that some dreams can take years to materialise, but they are also evidence that nothing or no one can stop the will and purpose of God, not even our own silly mistakes.

His father's favourite, his brothers, already hated the prophet and dreamer Joseph with a passion. But when the young, immature, teenager dared to suggest to his brothers that he had dreamed a dream and saw them one day bowing before him, the Bible says they hated him all the more.

Then, when he had another dream about how the sun, moon and eleven stars were bowing down to him and told his father, the Bible records how his brothers stripped him of his coat of many colours given to him by his father and then left their brother to die in a pit. They later sold him, as a slave into Egypt, where his life took a downward spiral beyond comprehension.

Have you ever been left to die in a pit by your own brethren? Ever found yourself in a tight spot? It was Joseph's experience. Having been abandoned by his brothers everything Joseph had dreamed of seemed lost. His hopes and aspirations had died in Egypt following false accusations of inappropriate advances towards Potiphar's wife; notwithstanding, after many years; God reignited his gift to dream again for when he was able to interpret the King's dreams, he was restored to a position of influence (Prime Minister) and brought out of the prison.

What does this suggest to us?

Two things: Firstly, it's important to dream, and secondly, God is a restoring God!

Don't allow small minds or difficulty to convince you that your dreams are too big, or not of value. And don't believe the lie that your goal has died, that your life is beyond the restoration of a loving and purposeful God.

Who told you to stop dreaming?

What has God promised you, and you've given up on it?

What were you aiming for before it got cruelly snatched from your grasp?

Maybe you are in debt, your marriage has failed, your kids have gone wild, and your world has imploded. Perhaps grief has left you badly traumatised. You may be in a personal prison right now, and that's hard, but who told you to stop dreaming? Who told you your life is over and you can't laugh, love and smile again?

Don't allow injury to derail you from God's purpose. It's been said that Satan's setbacks are frequently God's setups!

Trauma in the life of Naomi, probably was meant to stop her, but it would end up promoting her. Learn to view trouble and opposition like Joseph did — as a friend because often trouble will move you to your destiny. Isn't this what transpired in the life of Joseph — his problem became his transportation. It isn't easy, of course, to keep on dreaming and keep doing the right thing when the wrong thing is happening; when the roof is caving in around us, but that's what Joseph did, and that's what will help all of us attain our goals in life.

Despite unspeakable setbacks and opposition, Joseph remained focused, and kept on dreaming — he remained positive and kept calm. He retained the right attitude when the wrong things were happening. In the midst of disaster and enormous disappointment, he continued to do the God thing, not just the right thing. It's not easy to keep doing the right thing when the wrong thing is happening to you. The most significant test we face in life on a regular basis is the discouragement test. Life's not always fair, but if you keep doing the right thing, God will get you to where you are supposed to be. It's interesting how his brothers took Joseph's coat, but they couldn't take the calling on his life.

They left him penniless, but what does that matter when you're a prince with God, and God has a destiny planned for you?

In the same way, Naomi was penniless for a long time but *"the blessing of the Lord which makes rich and adds no sorrow with it"* (Proverbs 10:22) was waiting up ahead as God had always intended to restore what this faithful lady had lost.

Similar to Paul, Joseph, too, had learned in all things and places to be content. No matter what was taking place, he managed his position and continued to dream big.

Of course, Joseph is not the only Bible great to dream dreams. Daniel, Jacob, Paul, Joseph of Nazareth and many others had the experience of dreaming. Dreaming is a God thing, and most of God's servants have been great dreamers. This provokes a timely question: Is the Church still capable of God-given and divine dreams?

As Joseph walked towards his brothers in Dothan one day, plotting to kill him, they said: "Here comes that dreamer."

Talk about a prophecy and a compliment!

A dreamer he most certainly was, but he also had the gift of interpretation. His dreams were real, not "cheese and toast dreams"! They were true visions of the future, and, yet, like many God-inspired dreams it would take years to find fulfilment.

When the prophet Habakkuk went into his Watchtower to seek God's will for a nation, he was told to *"Write the vision and make it plain upon tables that he may run that readeth it. For the vision is for an appointed time, but at the end, it shall speak, and not lie, though it tarry, wait for it; because it will surely come, it will not tarry."* (Habakkuk 2:2-3)

When God gives you dreams, you may have to wait to see them come to pass, but it will be obvious they are from him; hence the importance of God's people and His church continuing to dream and believe in visions no matter how far this generation moves away from such a practice.

Solomon wrote; *"Where there is no vision the people perish"* (Proverbs 29:18). The ESV version explains it this way "When there is no prophetic revelation of God the people cast off restraint."

When the pastor, his people and the Church stop dreaming, they are in trouble. When there is no vision, there will be no progress, no direction and no revelation. Setbacks and negative situations will test our ability to keep dreaming, but those who allow God's spirit to prophesy of more magnificent days ahead will find new strength.

So it was with Naomi. Despite many hardships, this once positive, pleasant and beautiful woman began to dream big again in numerous and even in supernatural ways.

In misery and buried in Moab, her spirit started to revive. The Moabites, her sons, and Elimelech had previously told Naomi God didn't care; they had even questioned whether Naomi was following the right God in the first place. They mocked her faith, hopes and dreams and for a while, she believed this false report, but things were about to change.

Like Joseph, the anointing of God had never left her and was constantly at work in her life.

"Why is she not visiting the temple to seek the gods?" is what many Moabites might have muttered among themselves as she struggled to overcome the tragedy in her life. What they didn't understand, however, was that Naomi's God didn't reside in the temple, but deep within her heart. Again, like Joseph, God had put dreams and a purpose deep down inside her, and He would fulfil them in His time and for His glory.

As she fell asleep under the weight of her immense stress, those dreams finally started to kick in. She began to imagine a conversation with Mahlon before he passed away. It was dialogue that haunted her and continued to cause her anguish even many months after his passing.

She recalled how he was working in the field one day when Naomi asked him to take a break, but he reacted angrily. As she drifted back in time, recollecting the incident, she recalled every bit of it:

"You look exhausted, Mahlon; please rest my son and trust God."

"Trust God, after what happened to father and Chilion; you expect me to trust God? What is wrong with you, Mother?"

"Mahlon, your father may not have taught you the ways of God, he may not have believed in God the way he should have, but trust me, God is faithful, and He won't disappoint."

"Is that another one of those blind religious statements or do you believe that stuff, Mother?"

"All God is looking for, Mahlon, is for us to have faith."

"Faith? Have faith in what?

"Faith in the living God, Mahlon."

"How can I believe in a God who I can't see or hear? Father was a good father, I have been a good husband and look at what has happened to our family? Maybe our father was right, maybe the Moabites are right? Maybe this God you speak of is just a figment of your imagination?"

"Don't ever say that, Mahlon, our God is as real as we are standing here today."

If only Naomi could feel Mahlon back in her arms again; if only she could spend time with Chilion and Elimelech, too. The thought of never seeing her loved ones again was soul-destroying. Her heart was in mourning because she missed her husband, her sons and the reality of God in her life when they had all lived in Israel. Back then her faith was God-breathed, vibrant, exciting and alive, but Moab had left her dead, without hope and so utterly bereft.

Stirring briefly, angrily, and with bitterness, she cried out to God. "Why did you not take me? Why am I the only one left? What you are asking of me is too great. How can I dream of good things again? I can't live without the men in my life; I just can't, Lord".

An exhausted Naomi soon drifted off into another world of daydreams, but this one was special, an experience she never wanted to end. Suddenly, there he was — her beautiful Elimelech. It was him, wasn't it? He was just the same, her handsome Elimelech who had been so elegant and with such a kind disposition. Naomi immediately reached out and touched his face and hands. His smile was just like always. He hugged her and held her close. Only if he spoke with her, however, would she truly believe it was him?

"Listen to me, Naomi, I know things haven't worked out as you would have liked. I understand you are in grief and have genuine pain at present, but you will recover. It's only a matter of time. God has forgiven all of us for our mistakes. Never let anyone take your song or your dream, Naomi, because it's your song which brings strength and your song will defeat the enemy of your soul."

"You don't understand, Elimelech, not only have I lost you, but the boys are gone, too. It's a nightmare of all nightmares. Who could have believed this would happen to our family and me, a family who had everything? I miss you so much, Elimelech, and the boys. You are constantly on my mind. Oh, Elimelech, you can't imagine how much I miss you, my love..."

"I can, and where I am, trust me I understand everything now, Naomi, but you've got so much to look forward to, and you will find peace, love, and happiness again. Just keep going and don't give up. Allow yourself to love, laugh, live and hope again."

"I wish I could, Elimelech, believe me, I do, but I just can't at present."

None of this was real, of course, but when we are suffering even our imaginings can feel real and bring comfort. Quite often such thoughts prove both instructive and profitable. No matter how many times Naomi had tried to rationalise; the fact remained her circumstances made no sense and she could see no real prospects for her or the girls. Even though Elimelech had told her before he died, she was blameless and that it was his entire fault, Naomi had thus convinced herself that she alone was to blame for everything.

Is that why I feel so estranged from God?

Maybe God is punishing me for not doing more to stop this rash and thoughtless relocation?

I should have been stricter with Elimelech and told him to stop in his tracks.

Maybe it is my fault, after all?

Even in her imaginings, the guilt was there and the allegations. Those wild hallucinations, where she had sought refuge from self-recriminations day after day, had offered no real hiding place, no rest at all until suddenly voices of comfort arrived, and God was the speaker.

It had to be the Lord because the devil never speaks words of encouragement. That's how she knew it was God. To be back with Elimelech was such a wonderful feeling, but to meet again with her two departed children was a welcome moment, too and so why wouldn't she allow the dream to continue?

"Father is right. It's not your fault, Mother, and it never was. You must stop feeling guilty over something that was out of your control. God had a reason for taking the men in your life, even your closest loved ones. Try not to blame God, forgive yourself and start again."

"Thank you, Chilion; you were always such a kind young man. I remember in Israel when you were a little boy you could tell when I was feeling down. You would bring me something and curl up beside me, and it meant so much to me. If I could have taken your misery, I would have my son. It was hard for me to watch you hurt for most of your young life and then see you pass away like that."

"Chilion is right, Mother. You did your best; life is what it is. You say you believe in God; so believe in Him. Go on with God, worship Him and trust Him like you used to tell us to do and see where He takes you, yes even now, mother, watch and see what God will do."

"That's what I admire about you, Mahlon; you are the ultimate encourager and always spoke positive words to me. But things turned sour in Moab, and your spirit became so demoralised. I understand why you talked harshly to me before you died. I don't blame you at all. You were disappointed and devastated with how life had turned out. I felt so responsible for this and wish we could all turn the clock back."

"Well, I am speaking different words now, Mother. No one can turn back the clock and I know it will be hard, but you need to get up, and you need to go on. Things will work out, you will see".

As the voice of her son Mahlon slowly faded out, and she came to, it occurred to Naomi how she'd been sleeping through the night and dreaming something beautiful, something which forced her to confront her circumstances.

As she rose from her dream to the sight of the wall in front of her Naomi knew it was finally time to face her demons. That wall and the depression which had dogged her was a horrible reminder of just how far she still had to travel, yet those timely imaginary visits by Elimelech and her sons had convinced Naomi that God was both speaking to her and with her.

They had given her fresh hope and renewed strength. Was restoration possible and could it be birthed through something as simple as dreams?

She had always believed that God could speak through dreams and visions. He did it with Joseph of old and many other biblical greats, why not with her?

How about you?

Do you believe the power of dreams can restore the most unlikely of situations, even yours?

Do you believe that God can, and often does, bring good out of our poor choices? Are you entirely convinced that God is a restoring God?

God's grace is bigger and broader than our worst mistakes and He can meet us in the night watches. The dreams and hope He gives us help revive us and spur us on to the next chapters of our lives. According to Joel, God is still in the business of revealing Himself through the power of dreams and especially in these last days in which we live. He wrote; *"And it shall come to pass afterward, that I will pour out my spirit upon all flesh, and your sons and your daughters shall prophesy, your old men shall dream dreams, your young men shall see visions."* (Joel 2:28)

If God births a dream, He will bring it to pass, and no one is beyond His loving reach, even those of other religions.

For example, today many Muslims are testifying to how God has sent angels to their homes and districts to reveal the one true God — Jesus Christ? These life-changing incidents are happening regularly in the Middle-East and in many other places even without the help of any human form of evangelism. In the same way, despite the lessons learned from her life, no matter how big her mess, Naomi would have an even greater experience. She would discover that God is not just a God of dreams, but a God who turns those dreams into reality by restoring and healing the broken-hearted.

God is a restorer of broken situations and ruined lives!

Maybe you've made a life-altering choice like Elimelech, opportunities which have brought shame and pain to yourself and to others. The consequences may not have produced death, thanks to the goodness of a merciful God, but they caused your dreams to die, and the lives of people around you have been affected.

Are people unwilling to forgive you for that choice?

Are you struggling to forgive yourself?

Do you think God can't or won't forgive you?

The good news is God is merciful. He understands our weaknesses and our human frailties and wants to restore everything in the future. Your comeback may not reappear in the way you experienced previously, but God has a comeback planned for you and He has a million ways of making things up to you.

The book of Joel states; *"And I will restore unto you the years that the swarming locusts have eaten."* (Joel 2:25)

God can restore everything that's been stolen from your life and He can heal every hurt and every pain. Restoration is God's speciality and Naomi would be no exception. God was about to show her that He is a restorer of broken situations, broken dreams and ruined lives. He can replace what the enemy stole from you. Remember Jesus said; *"For the thief cometh not but for to steal, and to kill and to destroy, but I am come that you might have life and that they might have it more abundantly."* (John 10:10)

God will never give up on our dreams!

Even in her final dreams, it was as if Elimelech was speaking personally to Naomi for the last time; as though he was leaving her a concluding "goodbye message" imploring his wife to "get up" and "start again." It was as if he was the mouth of God leading her back to the will and purpose for her life.

She could hardly believe her eyes as Elimelech spoke softly with her. Tears rolled down her face when she imagined again those beautiful romantic coastal walks she once enjoyed with the love of her life. Hand in hand with her sweetheart, those were the days when she didn't have a care in the world.

Oh, how she missed him!

Oh, how she longed for him!

Oh, how welcome this dream was!

Elimelech used to call out to her at the shore and, cuddling her close, had reassured her everything was going to be fine.

If only things could be like that again?

Then, in her dream leaning over her chair, like a guardian angel with a life-changing message of love and encouragement, Elimelech breathed an instruction she would hug to her heart, words which would transform her destiny and bring enormous comfort to her soul.

"Everything is going to work out, Naomi. You're with me now."

As Elimelech pulled her close in, he reached over and softly planted a kiss on her little beauty spot, the one he'd always treasured.

"I will always be here for you, my precious Naomi; no one and nothing can separate us, not even death, and remember, you are not alone, and I am always with you."

"Oh, my precious Elimelech, just talking with you gives me hope and strength. Just hearing your voice picks me up. I love you."

"I love you, too, my beautiful and sweet Naomi, more than the moon, stars, and the sky. No one has ever touched my heart like you. In fact, did I ever tell you, Naomi, the day I set eyes on you was the best thing that ever happened to me and I'm thankful to God for that, but I need you to promise me you'll survive. Promise me that you won't give up, no matter what happens, no matter how hopeless it feels. I need you to promise me you're going to get up; you're going to live again, promise me that you'll never stop dreaming Naomi, and you'll never let go of that promise."

"I promise, you Elimelech, I promise, I'm going to live... my darling Elimelech, if that's what you want, you know what; I think I'm going to live."

Six

She Got Up

"So she got up with her daughters-in-law to return from the land of Moab, for in the land of Moab, she had heard that the Lord had visited His people by giving them food."
(Ruth 1:6)

For the first time in months, Naomi peered outside of a place which had become a prison — her home.

The sunlight was blinding, but it felt good to stare outside finally. Children were laughing and playing, a sign of life and hope for the future.

Just as well!

No matter how hard she might try, Naomi now knew she couldn't bring back her husband and sons. All her tears couldn't resurrect the dead in her life. Instead, she needed to focus on those who were still alive — herself, Ruth, and Orpah.

Life had passed her by, yet the girls had so much to look forward to. How could she expect them to go on caring for an older woman? Or to embrace what would in all probability be nothing other than a life of begging and poverty.

While no real ambition remained for Naomi, she clung to the dream of seeing Ruth and Orpah remarried and enjoying family life with their children.

That's why she must go back to her homeland and start again. Such a return was never far from her mind, it was always destined to happen.

We tend to gravitate towards the place where we are most comfortable, and Naomi had always felt safe and secure in Bethlehem.

She may have left Bethlehem with her husband and two sons during the famine, but Bethlehem had never left her.

What she needed, most, was a sign from God, a green light to go back and start again — a second chance!

Oh, that God would have mercy on her!

Oh, for an opportunity to put things right!

Have you ever longed for a second chance?

Ever wished you could go back and start all over again?

Ever messed up so badly you just wanted a clean slate and the opportunity to shine again?

Maybe you haven't messed up at all? Maybe circumstances rearranged the furniture in your life so dramatically it was out of your hands, yet you wish you could just go back and start all over again.

Starting all over again was the desire of Naomi's heart, too.

She'd proved how leaving God to follow what seemed right to the eyes brought only tragedy and heartache. The book of Proverbs states; *"There is a way that seemeth right to a man, but the end thereof are the ways of death."* (Proverbs 14:12)

Following the calamities she'd experienced in Moab there was only one road left to take for Naomi — the road back to Bethlehem. Further loss meant there was nothing to keep her in Moab? She had repented and now she wanted to return.

The Hebrew word Teshuva means repentance or return. Teshuva is not considered a single event in time but a process. Teshuva towards God is a journey with many acts of turning along the way, and with many highs and lows, a situation all of us are familiar with in our separate experiences with God, yet so often it takes a loving, merciful God to help begin our return and this is what transpired for Naomi.

As Naomi and the girls pottered about the house, a knock came to the door, a thump which sounded different from all the others. Usually, Naomi shied away from house callers, but this time expectancy arose in her heart. It was as if those dreams which included Elimelech, Mahlon, and Chilion had equipped her for this very moment. She was ready for it, but still petrified to answer.

"Someone's outside," Naomi shouted to the girls.

"I'll get it," replied Orpah, always eager to please her mother-in-law.

As Orpah greeted their guest, the sun streaked through their dark and dreary home like a ray of hope, a beautiful rainbow pouring through the hallway as a sign of brighter and better days to come. Welcome confirmation of the great mercy they were about to encounter. Standing there was an old friend of Naomi's from Israel who had travelled to bring some incredible news.

"We have a visitor, Naomi," Orpah shouted excitedly.

"Who is it?" Naomi enquired.

"Come and see; it's a man. He says he's an old friend of yours from Israel."

"Well, don't just stand there, bring him in."

As the man entered the room where Naomi had spent so many numerous lonely days, he embraced her with a hug and a smile.

"Naomi, how good it is to see you again. I bring you greetings from your homeland. We wondered what had become of you."

She could hardly believe who was standing in front of her. Avi was not just an old friend of hers, but also a dear colleague of her late husband, Elimelech.

"It's so nice to see you, Avi., What are you doing here?"

"Haven›t you heard, Naomi, God has been merciful and brought healing to our land. The famine is over, and the good times have returned. There is bread again in Israel. It's a miracle!"

Those words overwhelmed her, especially the words "there is bread again in Israel."

Her heart skipped a beat at the thought of having prayed so many times for revival of her beloved Israel, and now God had seemingly answered those prayers. It was music to her ears to learn how the Lord had revisited His people with food. Her day of deliverance had finally come, a day, she never thought possible.

"Come, Avi, and have something to eat with us," insisted Naomi.

"I would love to, Naomi, but I'm in a hurry. I only came to pass on my condolences for the loss of your husband and sons and to assure you we are praying for you and your family. I hope you know how much respect you still command in Bethlehem, and the people miss you so much."

"You'll never truly know how much that means to me, Avi. I appreciate your kind words and please pass on my best wishes to everyone in Bethlehem. I can't convey to you how much I have missed them too."

"The people miss you so much"... "the people miss you so much."

Those words touched the heart of Naomi more than anything. How she'd longed for her people. They were her brethren, her brothers and sisters, her dearest and closest family. She had always assumed they'd be angry with her for choosing to move elsewhere with her husband and children at a time when her people and homeland were struggling. On the contrary, this message from Avi was proof of how her people still loved and cared for her. If forgiveness was required, then it had already been offered.

The loving concern and support from her brethren back home confirmed that her time in Moab was over. A new season had arrived, a new chapter, here was the moment for Naomi to get up and return to her beloved Israel. This was the way God wanted her to walk in.

Orpah and Ruth raised their eyebrows at the news Naomi had received.

It was genuinely miraculous to them both, given what they had heard about the state of Israel and the hopelessness Naomi and her family had encountered previously.

Like the children of Israel before they crossed over the Jordan, God was about to do wonders for Naomi. He would meet her need in a way she could never have imagined, but not just yet and only if she played her part, for just as the children of Israel were required to show faith by trusting God and stepping out through the waters, Naomi too needed to take a step of faith to release a miracle in her life. If she genuinely wanted restoration, if she genuinely wanted change, she would have to rise and shine and get up from her self-made grave. Like Jonah who ended up in the belly of a fish, before finally agreeing to return to Nineveh, Naomi would first have to humble herself and return to the place of God's purpose for her life — the House of Bread.

God had brought her a sign of hope — bread was in abundance again in Israel, but Naomi would need to go after it! With the curse of famine replaced with the blessing of the Lord, deep down she knew it was time to return to her place of birth and the land of her ancestors.

Sometimes God's will is not as difficult to unravel as is often portrayed. For example, not always, but many times His will is where there is bread, both physically and spiritually.

While Avi had been referring to the bread which feeds our stomach, Naomi could just as easily have been considering the bread of life — the Word of God. She was a spiritual woman, and due to her heart-breaking and turbulent experiences, she understood more than ever that man cannot live by bread alone but as she had been taught, by every word God speaks.

Even more than natural food, the thing she had missed most during their exile in Moab was what Jesus would later describe in the New Testament as "the bread of life." Naomi knew that without this bread, her soul would never feel truly satisfied.

Jesus later said; *"I am the bread of life. Whoever comes to me will never go hungry, and whoever believes in me will never be thirsty."* (John 6:35)

Many nations are starving today due to a natural food shortage, yet a famine of God's word is equally serious.

It brings chaos and confusion and paralyses nations and individuals. Without the bread of life homes and lives are destroyed, and people are left malnourished and blessing decreases.

It not only happened in Elimelech's time but during other dark periods in history.

In the days of Samuel, the Bible describes how there was "no open vision" — a reference to a lack of bread and the preaching of the Word in God's house.

Solomon wrote; *"Without a vision, the people perish"*, and here indeed was a picture of Naomi during her days in Moab — a perishing woman with no future for her or her daughters-in-law.

It wasn't only a shortage of food and water which brought Naomi low, the absence of God's Word in a godless, heathen land, and the absence of His presence had equally left her spirit parched, stripping her of all hope.

What she longed for most now was a crust of God's living Word again, a crumb for her crisis and the unexpected and timely visit by Avi had created it.

He'd offered hope to a desperate woman living in a hopeless place. Naomi had become all-too-aware of the lack of the presence of Almighty God in her life. Those brutal years in Moab had taken a toll. Like David, when he lost the presence of God and cried; *"Restore unto me the joy of thy salvation."* (Psalm 51:12) so, too, Naomi was desperate to feel the same presence and anointing of God again in her life.

How indeed she longed for the sense of God's company again! She had missed the intimacy of Elimelech, the feel of his loving arms around her and the touch of his lips, yet it suddenly occurred to her how it also seemed ages since she felt God's nearness and approval. To lose the love of a husband was one thing, but to be unable to feel God's love while buried deep in a foreign land had proved even worse.

Back in Israel, that presence and special anointing was so tangible until, without warning, one day the dove of peace seemed to fly away. Naomi continued to worship in Moab, but there's a difference between experiencing the moving of the spirit and merely going to church. Naomi had come to believe that the former days couldn't be bettered or improved upon, both in her physical and spiritual life. She saw her life as being over. Life had stopped when worship stopped, and her dreams had ended when Elimelech and her sons died, yet her Creator had other ideas.

No matter how good things have been before, more magnificent days and greater things are still possible with God. Today there are multitudes of people who have lost hope and stopped attending the house of God; people who have simply given up like Naomi. These people were once filled with the Spirit of God but are now living in Moab and running on empty. Many reasons explain this demise, but one more prominent cause is likely — the absence of fresh bread (the Word of God) in the house of God. Israel and the true church of Jesus Christ cannot hope to survive without the bread of life. It's counterfeit to believe that sermons which are more original, creative, and intelligent are better than addresses based solely on the bread of life. Many reasons are cited for the obvious deficiency of people at church in this generation — too many distractions, apostasy and the lukewarm generation that we live in, yet only when there is bread again in the church will the masses begin to return, and the spirit begin to move again. Only when the true gospel is preached can revival take place,

Church growth is about more than strategy. The Bible reminds us how *"the anointing"* breaks every yoke (Isaiah 10:27).

Numbers swell and faith increases when anointed preaching takes place in God's house. In the words of the Apostle Paul; *"Faith comes by hearing and hearing by the word of God."* (Romans 10:17)

Today people are spiritually starved due to a lack of fresh bread, something which is backed by recent statistics. In the past decade, church attendance in the UK is thought to have decreased by fifty percent; notwithstanding, the same people who have walked away can yet be encouraged to return and be filled again by looking to Jesus and finding a church which believes that still the *"gospel is the power of God unto salvation."* (Romans 1:16)

Gimmicks and stunts can never compare to the preaching of the Word of God. Nothing can satisfy the soul like the word of truth. Jesus said; *"I am the bread of life, whoever comes to me shall not hunger, and whoever believes in me shall never thirst."* (John 6:35)

Naomi was not just weak in body; she was down in her spirit because of a lack of spiritual bread in the land of Moab, a shortage of God's holy word meant she had to address this deficit in her life.

Are you struggling at present due to a lack of spiritual bread?

Maybe you have lost God's sense of nearness by being too long in Moab. God longs for you to draw close to Him again.

Zechariah wrote; *"Return unto me saith the Lord and I will return unto you."* (Zechariah 1:3)

When Elimelech set out with his wife Naomi and the boys for Moab, they entered a downward spiral from which only Naomi, due to the grace of God, had survived. She was determined to get back up again.

It may sound obvious, but no one can get up unless they have first been down.

Naomi had been down in the dirt and the dust of despair, but now God was challenging her to rise and return to a place where bread was again plentiful, both in the physical and spiritual. We know we are in the will of God when we have overcome trials and tragedy, and there is food in our bellies and food on our spiritual table too. In this respect, Naomi is a picture of Israel and the church and even our generation. She was an ordinary person who went through extraordinary things and still made it out alive and got back up again.

Many people today have endured horrendous suffering similar to Naomi, and one should never underestimate the pain involved in those particular situations, but God is challenging these dear souls also to rise and get back up and return to their spiritual place. Since 9/11, considerable grief and loss have been echoed by many other unspeakable events — nationally, internationally, privately and publically, paralysing people of all backgrounds. It has been a complicated and painful path to recovery for thousands of these individuals, but across nations, adults and children have somehow found the courage to go on, to get back up again and to believe God for the future.

None of these brave individuals got up from nothing, of course. They had to find every ounce of strength and courage to rise from the ashes of unexpected and unfair bereavement, devastation injustice and even hopelessness. Poignantly, each year on the anniversary of their tragic events, such people have a choice; to move on or be held captive by the past.

Often anniversaries trigger physical and emotional pain, shock, horror and memories of the traumatic day. They are evidence of the way our bodies and minds register traumatic events, leaving imprints, even years afterwards.

In the same way, every year Naomi would have recalled the sorrowful experiences when she lost the three men in her life. She, too, had a choice: to remain in the past or grab the opportunity to remember, revisit, mourn and integrate an unlikely event with a stronger self. That wouldn't have been easy. Naomi, more than most, experienced a tragedy, which reshaped her world forever — the unexpected loss of her loved ones.

She required more than self-determination, this forlorn woman needed the love and support of others also to recover fully. Naomi had been distressed for some time and, like many victims of trauma, didn't get up immediately, but eventually.

What made her rise from the ashes?

When did Naomi decide to get up finally?

What provoked her to turn the corner so-to-speak?

She got up when she heard there was bread again in Israel.

She revived when hope returned.

She got up when she had honestly appraised her situation and decided "enough was enough!"

She got up when it was time for her to get up.

She was sick of depression, sick of self-pity, sick of defeat and living in the past. She couldn't stick her wretched circumstances another day longer.

Of course, no one can rise if they don't know where they are going.

Having a purpose and plan helps us to get back up and move forward, and in this respect Naomi's old acquaintance Avi brought more than bread and hope, he'd brought direction, clarity and a destination. Through him, God had spoken to Naomi with the words of Isaiah saying; *this is the way walk ye in it."* (Isaiah 30:21) and regardless of the apprehension she felt, Naomi was determined to follow the leading of the Lord.

Going on in life is always a choice, and Naomi chose to keep going on.

She showed courage and faith to help propel her forward when defeat and despair were pushing her backwards.

Her prayers were necessary, but only when she decided "enough is enough" did things begin to change.

What we tolerate we cannot change!

Luke says of the prodigal; *"and when he came to himself, he picked himself up and said, How many of my father's hired men have more than enough bread, but I am dying here with hunger!"* (Luke 15:17)

No one else did it for him. He had utterly humiliated and dishonoured his father, yet he still got up and returned to his father's house. If anyone felt forsaken it was Naomi and for a good reason, but even in the midst of her bleak environment, despite her adverse situation, she still believed God loved her and continued to place her faith in Him.

She accepted she had become bitter but was determined to get better.

She knew that to survive she simply must get back up.

The book of Ruth puts it like this; *"So she got up with her daughters-in-law to return from the land of Moab, for in the land of Moab, she had heard that the Lord had visited His people by giving them food."* (Ruth 1:6) She didn't get up by herself; she got up with the help of others — her daughters-in-law.

When Naomi, like the prodigal, considered the poverty she was in and the loss, she had suffered in Moab; when she reflected on the past number of years away from her homeland of Israel and brethren, family and friends, rising up, and going back home was a "no-brainer". Her path unfolded naturally before her. She needed to accept that no matter what the reasons were, her family had made huge mistakes moving in the first place and, despite the lateness of the hour, she became more determined than ever to correct them.

Naomi hadn't experienced a moment's blessing from the time they'd all left Israel and so as they bid farewell to Avi and wished him well, she clearly understood how his visit had been divinely orchestrated and for a great purpose — to inform her there was bread again in Israel. Avi had been sent by the most High God to prompt and direct Naomi to return to a land which had always held her heart — the land of her birth — a habitation she should never have left in the first place.

Seven

Turning Point

*"She set out from the place where she had been, with
her two daughters in law, and they went on their
way to return to the land of Judah."* (Ruth 1:6)

Decision made, Naomi had no guarantee that a better life
was waiting for her in Bethlehem than Moab, but her course
became set, even though things are quite different when we
return after long spells away. Missionaries say the hardest part
of their calling is not the going out; it's the returning home
again. Friends move on; new developments appear, the entire
fabric of society alters, and family can become scattered.

How many folks, for example, survived the famine Naomi
and Elimelech had escaped?

She had no idea!

While she and Elimelech had sought the more fertile
ground of Moab, many would have struggled and even
perished in Bethlehem all those years ago. How would the
survivors of such a bleak period in Israel's history feel about
the return of the prodigal daughter?

Avi had told Naomi she was welcome, but perhaps not
everyone would have been delighted at her arrival. Her
enemies may not have been gathering to stone her, but
Naomi would have felt the cold shoulder from some. With
no livelihood in Bethlehem either, it was a huge risk moving

back, but "there's no place like home", and Naomi's home was
definitely in Bethlehem. Besides, if this were God's will for
her life, then He would make a way; He would provide for her
needs and make the path smooth.

After her old friend Avi had brought her the news of how
prosperity had returned to Israel, her mind recalled how
the meaning of the name of her beloved town Bethlehem —
"House of Bread."

How the Promised Land seemed so inviting again, so
right.

Hadn't bread returned?

Hadn't God's blessing been restored?

Hadn't the hand of God's mercy touched her life again?

Prosperity and provision and spiritual blessings were the
order of the day once again so naturally, Naomi couldn't wait
to go back and see it with her own eyes.

Mind you, it did seem precarious following the guidance
of God because there's always a risk where considerable
change and upheaval is involved but obeying human instincts
hadn't proved any more successful in the past for Naomi.

Also, Orpah and Ruth required her to be more positive
and think of them — young women with the rest of their
lives ahead. They couldn't remain as they were, moping
over mistakes and disappointments, all-be-it; they had all
suffered cruel bereavement in their lives. Instead they faced
a watershed moment, a crossroads and even a crisis moment
of truth forcing them into action.

"It was a turning point in his career" is something that's
said of someone who manages to go from a negative to a
favourable situation, although the opposite can also transpire.
Turning points are welcome when they produce a positive

outcome, but Naomi's turning point did not indicate this. She had no guarantees that by leaving Moab and returning to her birth land of Israel that things would be any better and her dilemma was made even harder by having to return to the place she'd left.

It is a humbling experience when a turning point becomes a returning point!

Like Hagar, headed for Egypt and on the run from the house of Abraham and Sarah, pregnant with Abraham's child, notwithstanding God sent angels to block her path and commanded her to return to the place she'd left. It was a place of pain and rejection, especially by Sarah, Abraham's jealous and barren wife. In all probability, it would have been humiliating having to return to the scene of the crime so-to-speak, a home where Hagar had suffered considerable persecution and injustice, but sometimes God asks us to do the seemingly impossible. It was so with Naomi. Instead of heading in the direction of somewhere new, she was prompted by the Almighty to return to the old, in particular, her old stomping ground of Bethlehem. Naomi had to face the fact that things hadn't worked out for her or her family in Moab. The entire journey had proved a nightmare from start to finish, and things were not getting any better. She needed to accept the truth that God was leading her back to a place she'd abandoned with her husband all those years ago.; a location she was born and grew up; a place she loved deep within her heart, yet a location and people she hadn't been part of for some years.

Going forward to find our destiny is one thing; going back is quite another, and this was Naomi's quandary.

Naomi was all too conscious of the fact that her daughters-in-law were worse off staying with her in Moab. They had family and would gladly be welcomed home again to a much more comfortable environment, one they hadn't enjoyed for some time. She sat chatting with her daughters, appearing miles away in her thoughts, even though her face seemed radiant with peace and joy signifying a unique turning point in her condition.

Here was the moment she'd dreamed of, the chance to start again in her old stomping ground, but how would she explain her decision to return to Israel to her faithful and loyal daughters in law? She couldn't hide it from them any longer.

"Girls, I've something to share with you. I've decided to go back to Israel and Bethlehem. I'm packing today because I believe God has made the way clear for me to return. The famine in Israel is over, and there's no future for me here. I want to put the past behind me and begin a new life with my people."

Naomi had feared to tell the girls, but her words brought surprising positivity from both Orpah and Ruth.

"That's wonderful news! It's what you need, Mother. I've watched all these years, and it's clear your heart has never truly left your homeland. I'm so glad you've made this courageous decision," Ruth insisted.

"Really, and there was me thinking I'd done a good job becoming a Moabitess and blending in with your culture, Ruth."

"A Moabitess, Mother? Don't make me laugh? You, of all people, could never pass for that."

Ruth was right. Naomi had tried to fit in, having decided to make a go of it in Moab, but had always looked like a "fish out of water" and well out of her comfort zone.

Orpah sniggered in approval at Ruth's remarks before giving Naomi a ringing endorsement. "I don't know your God, Mother, but it's obvious to me this is what He wants for you. You've never been happy in Moab because your heart has always been in Bethlehem. I agree with Ruth; I think this is a wonderful decision. Let's all pack together."

"Wow, wow, wow, slow down, no one said anything about you girls coming with me. Not for a moment do I expect either of you to accompany me back to Bethlehem. Moab is your homeland and culture. It would be unreasonable of me to expect you to leave the land of your birth. Besides our laws and ways are so different in Israel that it would make it impossible for you to serve the gods of Moab."

"That's rich coming from you, Mother," replied Ruth. "I seem to recall how you came here from another culture and country."

"True, Ruth, but it hasn't been easy. I wouldn't recommend those experiences to anyone, and I don't want the same thing happening to either of you two girls."

"We are coming with you, mother and that's the end of the matter," insisted Ruth.

Naomi was having none of it. She paused, took the hand of Ruth and whispered gently. "You've always been so sweet and thoughtful, Ruth, a wonderful daughter. There have been times when I didn't know how I could have coped without you, but I'm sorry I cannot allow it. You must remain in Moab and rebuild your lives. Think about it; you are still young enough to remarry and have children of your own. Imagine being lumbered with a widow like me in what would be a strange land to you both?"

Ruth responded angrily, "Have you forgotten something, Mother; we are all family now? We will not leave you or let you go without us."

Orpah wept and declared, "Ruth is right, Mother, we will not leave you, ever!"

Knowing the trauma Naomi had endured, they couldn't abandon a woman so loving to them both and deeply traumatised and haunted by the past? Naomi not only required company but human support to help her make a proper recovery. Having experienced immense calamity and ordeal in her life, in all probability she'd slipped into some form of depression. No one loses a husband and two children and walks away unscathed. Yes, Naomi was a child of God, but grief is a natural response to losing someone or something important to us, and we may feel a variety of emotions, like sadness and loneliness. These emotions emerge when a loved one dies; a relationship ends or due to the loss of a job or long-term experience. Other life changes like chronic illness or a move to a new home can also lead to unhappiness and apprehension. Everyone mourns differently, but it's common for people left bereaved and those without closure to life-shattering incidents to go through long spells of lockdown caused by trauma.

Naomi may have lived in a different generation, but she would have endured all of the stages of grief associated with Post Traumatic Stress Disorder (PTSD), such as denial, anger, guilt, depression, and even acceptance and who could blame her? Naomi's world was turned upside down in the most unexpected manner, and in the way, many are experiencing today. Consider some of the things people in this generation or perhaps even you have had to witness, things such as war, poverty, and terrorism?

No one is immune to such things.

Returning war heroes and Christian missionaries are among those most affected by PTSD. We see on TV, and in the newspaper, and on social media, terrible cases of what soldiers of war and soldiers of the cross have had to endure in foreign lands. It's important to state how such traumatic events don't only wound our mind; such combat abroad and catastrophic incidents at home can equally leave a lasting effect on our soul, too.

The implications of experiencing or seeing a terrifying or unpleasant event must not be underestimated. We are all spiritual beings on a physical journey. For some, that journey has led to incredible trauma and pain, experiences which have left a mark that changed the way they see the world. Harrowing encounters can wound not only our body and mind, but also our souls. The book of Psalms records; *"Why are you cast down, oh my soul and why are you in turmoil within me? Hope in God, for I shall again praise him, my salvation and my God."* (Psalm 43:5)

Many of us spend the majority of our lives trying to manage and treat symptoms such as anger, depression, sleeplessness, relationship dysfunction, or substance abuse. We may have used therapy, prescription medication, or self-medication to reduce the impact of those symptoms on our day-to-day lives, yet life hasn't got any better. In fact, things may be getting worse. That's because it's no longer our bodies and minds that are impacted, but the pain is now deep rooted within our souls.

People frequently seek peace for their minds when, in fact, it's their souls which are troubled.

The prophet Jeremiah wrote; *"Stand ye in the ways and see and ask for the old paths, where is a good way, and walk therein, and ye shall find rest for your souls, but they said we will not walk therein."* (Jeremiah 6:16)

How then did Naomi begin any form of the recovery process when she was suffering from a broken heart and crushed soul? She began to retrace her steps with the help and kindness of others and the support of genuine brethren around her.

Regardless of how strong you are, some battles require a greater force, not a single warrior. No man is an island. The Bible reminds us how, *"One shall chase a thousand but two shall put ten thousand to flight."* (Deuteronomy 32:30)

Today there are organisations which specialise in providing support and help to those who are suffering from depression and trauma, and the majority of these excellent organisations focus on interaction and human comfort; Naomi found this same comfort in the form of her two daughters-in-law, Ruth and Orpah. God did not expect her to endure the pain alone, nor did He in any way leave her comfortless.

Solomon said; *"And though a man might prevail against one who is alone, two will withstand him — a threefold cord is not quickly broken."* (Ecclesiastes 4:12)

God will send what is needed to strengthen you and it won't necessarily be who you expect. For example, it wasn't well-known Israelites who helped steer the ailing Naomi back to her homeland. It wasn't her former brethren or two children of God; instead, it was two foreign girls who gave her the help and support when she needed it most. These girls recognised the weakness of body and spirit their mother in law was experiencing and got to work to help during her time of greatest need.

The book of Exodus records; *"When Moses' hands grew tired, they took a stone and put it under him, and he sat on it. Aaron and Hur held his hands up — one on one side, one on the other, so that his hands remained steady till sunset."* (Exodus 17:12)

Of course, at this point, neither of these two girls professed faith in Jehovah God but that didn't mean God couldn't use them both to bless and help strengthen Naomi and get her from Moab to Israel in one piece.

God can use who He wants when He wants and how He wants.

Isaiah writes; *"For my thoughts are not your thoughts, neither are your ways my ways, saith the Lord."* (Isaiah 55:8)

Who would have imagined how God would use Joseph to save his family and a nation from starvation by bringing them to one of their enemies, Egypt of all places? Only God could have planned Joseph's elevation to the position of Prime Minister giving him incredible authority and power in the land of Egypt.

Would anyone have chosen a Hebrew slave like Moses who was rescued as a baby from the river Nile to be the deliverer of the children of Israel, again in the land of Egypt?

How about a little girl named Esther who stood in the gap with prayer and fasting for her people, saving them from the evil plan of Haman who desired to destroy the Jewish people.

And think about it!

Naomi had not one, but two foreign daughters-in-law, both of whom had nothing in common with her, yet both of whom God had assigned to comfort her following her disappointments. No one travels this road successfully alone. No one makes it back from illness or grief single handily. We all need each other, and Naomi needed the help of her two faithful daughters.

Who has God placed in your life to be a blessing to you? They may not be what you expected, their religious beliefs may be different and the colour of their skin, even their cultural understanding and background, but don't reject them in case you reject the blessing of the Lord.

Both Ruth and Orpah were all too aware of Naomi's previous struggles. Naomi had swapped a position of affluence and even authority in Israel to follow a new path in life, but after the move to Moab she became entirely overwhelmed by her new environment. It didn't turn out anything like she was expecting. She was a "fish out of water" struggling to adapt to her new country and new conditions and with every new tragedy she could feel her life spiralling out of control. Her financial status had dropped considerably, but there was an even larger issue — she'd lost her friends, brethren, place of familiarity; her self-esteem and confidence and her entire identity. Because she'd always "dug in" during difficult times previously, Naomi assumed this approach would work again, but to her shock and horror, it didn't. Instead, for the first time in her life she was overcome with grief and emotion.

Making matters worse was the fact that she wrongly believed that God's people shouldn't get depressed or become defeated, especially prominent people. She'd always been strong before so when that same strength wasn't forthcoming, suddenly neither was the answers. Depression was for weak people and if she had the spirit of God living inside her, then she shouldn't be depressed about anything. Bottling everything up she hid what she perceived as 'personal shame' from her daughters in law, friends and everyone she met. She refused help and support due to pride, embarrassment and a place she'd never been in before.

Naomi would visit the temple and smile and pretend everything was okay, but inwardly she was struggling beyond words. She would joke and laugh at public gatherings and then go home and cry her heart out. She would project the most positive image outside, while feeling anything but positive inside.

Naomi's life had become a complete sham and a shamble.

Only when her daughters drew alongside to help did she begin to admit the problem she was having and start to consider her position.

God has his angels and helpers everywhere, but it is up to us to recognise and accept them. The book of Hebrews states; *"Be not forgetful to entertain strangers, for thereby some have entertained strangers unawares."* (Hebrews 13:2)

The New Living Bible translation of this verse is; *"Don't forget to show hospitality to strangers, for by so doing some people have shown hospitality to angels without realising it!"* (Hebrews 13:2)

On reflection, this season of uncertainty was a horrible period in the life of Naomi, but she still learned an incredibly valuable lesson; God reveals Himself through the compassion and kindness of others.

We all require help during our darkest days, and God often sends unexpected angels who specialise in providing us with exactly what we require.

Naomi was no exception; she too, found added strength and regained her direction with the help and love of two precious angels — her two daughters-in-law. They made her turning point easier to navigate. They helped her to defeat her demons and overcome her grief. They instilled severely needed confidence in her and encouraged her to keep going. And yet they were from Moab!

They remained faithful to her regardless of any religious barriers and were of great consolation to this single mother. The men in her life may have died, but God hadn't abandoned her or left her without support.

So often bereavement and injustice focus on what is lost, not on what remains, yet God, in His great love, mercy, and infinite wisdom, will always send the broken and bereaved a comforter to lead them to a new and exciting pathway.

Has your life experienced extreme turmoil?

Do you feel tired and weary?

Is your soul downcast like Naomi's?

Have you reached a turning point?

David wrote in the well-known Psalm 23; *"The Lord is my Shepherd, I shall not want. He makes me lie down in green pastures; he leadeth me beside the still waters. He restoreth my soul."* (Psalm 23:1-3)

God specialises in making our steps a little more comfortable, and He knows who to use to help renew our souls.

Eight

Going Back to Go Forward

"Choose this day whom you will serve, but as for me and my house, we will serve the Lord." (Joshua 24:15)

There is an old saying: Never go back. It's often true but not always and certainly not in the case of Naomi.

They set off on foot early next morning, the wind gusting, and the mountains near Moab striking in the background, but nothing was more attractive to Naomi than catching the first sight of her beloved Israel.

She was beside herself at the prospect of returning to the land of her birth and, naturally, filled with anxiety, too. The thought of going back to a place where she had so many precious memories would have been uppermost in her mind. Naomi had an overabundance of unanswered questions. How would Bethlehem look now? Was her former hometown still prospering? Were the folks as happy and close as when she'd left all those years ago? How was the place where they used to worship? Were her friends and relatives still there? Did they overcome the famine, or did it decimate their homes and livelihoods? Come to think of it; would she be received or rejected by her people?

To feel and breathe the air of Israel again was all she sought. To be home would make every problematic step there worth it all. It was Naomi's only hope in life now, to be dwelling again with her loved ones and to die in the place of her birth. Her one remaining desire was to put to bed, once

and for all, the awful memory of her experiences in Moab.
But first, they would all have to endure the dusty, windy road
in front of them which seemed long and daunting. She and
the girls remained focused as they fought the stiff breeze in
their faces. Naomi refused to look back, mainly because she'd
no intentions of going back. Go back to what - misery and
pain and the absence of God's beautiful presence?

Not a chance!

Here was a woman on a mission — a mission to return
home to her fellow countrymen and culture. Pressing into
the wind Naomi set her face towards Jerusalem. Like Jesus
who set his face as a flint towards Jerusalem when going to
the cross, so Naomi focused on one purpose to return to the
land of her birth and people.

Words were few and far between them all as they
journeyed, although thoughts were plenteous until
finally Ruth broke the ice.

"Are you looking forward to arriving in Bethlehem,
Mother?"

Naomi remained tight lipped. Instead, head
down to protect her from the swirling wind; she kept
walking; her eyes fixed on her destination; as if she
was in a race against time — and in many ways she
was. That horrible memory of Moab was haunting her
every step. Carrying a large bag filled with grain and
water; she harboured a burden few other women have
ever experienced. She hadn't brought any material
items with her. Instead, Naomi preferred the simple
things in life to the regalia of the Moabites.

Orpah was different, however. She carried
everything, while simple Ruth brought a small bag of
essentials like her mother in law.

"Maybe the wind is too strong, and she can't hear you," remarked Orpah to Ruth.

So Ruth persisted, "What's the matter, Mother. Is something wrong?"

Naomi sighed, and then stopped in her tracks. She'd assumed the eagerness of her two daughters to follow her back to Bethlehem was nothing more than misguided loyalty, and the exuberance of youth, and they would return once the journey had gotten underway. The enormity of leaving their families behind in Moab would dawn upon them eventually? Naomi genuinely hadn't expected the girls to stay with her, and so faced quite a dilemma. Should she put up with their company a while longer or was it time to speak the truth to both of them?

Quickly turning around Naomi began, "Yes, yes, something is wrong. Something is very wrong. I'm sorry, I know we've discussed it, but you both must go back to Moab. I am returning to Israel to find favour with God again, but you are different. You are both not to blame for anything that happened in Moab and remember I'm not your real mother; you must go back to your families. How will I support you both?"

Ruth was having none of it. Sensing the grief-stricken heart of her mother-in-law who was feeling the pangs of despair and loneliness, Ruth refused to back down.

"You have been more of a mother to us than our real parents, and you have taken great care of us — care we can never repay. To leave you now is unthinkable."

Naomi's eyes filled to the brim, and her heart felt like it would explode. She could sense the concern and compassion in her daughters-in-law. She didn't want to part with them, but that was her plan. She had expected to say goodbye on route to her homeland, but she would never forget her two daughters-in-law, and she had already vowed to God to pray continually for them both.

Naomi stopped again. "I love you both, very much, but please don't worry about me; I will be all right, girls. Please, I beg you, return to your homes. The Lord will bless you both for your loyalty to your husbands and me. Do this for me and do it now."

Ruth sharply rebuked her mother-in-law, contending, "No, I will not return, no way are we leaving you. Don't ask me to do this, Naomi."

Suddenly Orpah became silent and her demeanour changed from sincere to sheepish. Prompted by the frightening reality of life in a new country and culture and torn by the thought of having to leave her homeland, the truth of the situation finally began to hit home to Orpah, especially as Naomi had given Orpah a way out. Going back would be her "escape clause" for deep within her heart she had never truly wanted to go to Israel in the first place. Her loyalty was misplaced. It was towards Naomi, there was no doubt about that; she cared for her mother-in-law, but not for Naomi's God.

As she remained silent, even troubled, during the exchanges, Naomi and Ruth sensed Orpah's apprehension.

"Is everything alright, Orpah," asked Naomi.

Was Orpah as committed as she had once professed to be?

Or, was this dyed-in-the-wool Moabitess genuinely contemplating going back to Moab,

Maybe her mother-in-law was right all along. Perhaps the change of culture was indeed too much for Orpah to endure. How would she find a husband in a place like Bethlehem? She would stand out like a sore thumb there. Imagine the stigma involved. Was she ready to give up the gods of Moab for an unknown God she had never believed?

And, like Naomi had said, what future would there be trying to look after a penniless, ageing widow like Naomi, especially when Orpah herself might end up rejected and poor? Orpah, who had deep down always trusted in the flesh, had never been convinced that anything good could come out of Israel. She had said so on numerous occasions. She and Ruth fought many times about Naomi's claims to serve the one true God. And, in the end, Orpah's true colours emerged. She cared more for herself than others and never believed she would get blessed in Israel. Just like Nathanael who asked Phillip the question; *"Can any good thing come out of Nazareth?"* (John 1:46), Orpah continually doubted the existence of Jehovah God and all things Israel, and, as a result, on lots of occasions had fought with Ruth over religion, Israel, and the gods of Moab.

Resembling Lot, her forefather, Orpah was a double-minded individual more influenced by her flesh than the spirit of the living God. Similar, also, to Lot's wife, who eventually perished when she looked back and turned into a pillar of salt, Orpah appears to have preferred to gaze at the things of the flesh, returning to Moab, rather than moving forward in faith and experiencing the joys of the spirit?

The name Orpah is recalled by Jewish tradition as "one who turned back", which ultimately, she decided to do. The Midrash even added how she became the ancestress of the

Philistine warrior, Goliath! A little cruel, but we get the picture.

Holy Scripture, however, does not attempt to condemn or blame Orpah for her return to Moab.

Why?

God gives all of us a choice to follow our hearts and to live our lives according to our conscience, nevertheless it's interesting to note how Orpah still chose to abandon Naomi when the opportunity presented itself. Remember, just a short time before this, Orpah had wept in the house and promised to follow Naomi wherever she went, yet when push came to shove; her heart was held captive by the gods of Moab. To Naomi and Ruth and even the outside world, her actions may have proved surprising, but her spirit had never fully surrendered to Israel and Jehovah.

There are people like this in Christendom today. They run well for a while, promise the earth, vowing to serve the pastor, the church, and the Lord, but in the long run, their selfish desires prevail. The attraction of remaining in Moab and finding another husband was too much for Orpah to resist.

Orpah couldn't escape from the pull of where she came from. She went back to all things familiar, back to bury her dead and to dead things because she found safety in her home patch. From the beginning, she had no real desire to follow her mother-in-law, even though she loved and respected her. Orpah's loyalty always belonged to her family of birth, not Naomi's family of God. "Blood is thicker than water", is an old saying and this was Orpah. All along, there had been a doubt; all along two hearts were living under one roof; all along the heart of Orpah represented the flesh; but by contrast, the heart of Ruth represented the Spirit of God.

Ruth ran in the direction of her dream, Orpah followed the direction of her disease.

She had the opportunity of a lifetime staring her in the face, the opportunity to come to Israel and find Jehovah God, but she still returned to where she'd come from.

Imagine arriving at the door of your delivery, about to move into the blessing of the Lord, about to find eternal salvation and security, then deciding it's too risky and going back to the bondage you had experienced for most of your life?

In this respect, is Orpah any different from many people today? God is offering them hope but they prefer hopelessness, He offers them life, but they instead choose death.

Orpah knew how to survive in Moab, she understood the laws and rules of the land, she knew how to function there, so she blew her opportunity in Bethlehem through fear of the future and familiarity with the past.

Are you Orpah or Ruth? Are you comfortable around death, sinfulness and apathy or do you desire blessing, honour and accomplishment?

Are you willing to follow your dreams, or have you decided to go back and bury your dead?

Orpah's husband died, her father-in-law died, her brother-in-law died, yet she ran back to the environment of death and destruction. Are you remaining with dead things?

Naomi had always perceived this weakness in Orpah, and so implored her to return to the home of her parents where she would feel so much happier and comfortable. Immediately she agreed, gathering her things, not even turning around to wave goodbye. Naomi gave Orpah her blessing and a choice, and Orpah chose to return to her former life. So it is with God.

No one is forced to love or follow God.

Elijah told the people in the book of kings; *"How long will you halt between two opinions? If the Lord be God, follow him, but if Baal, then follows him."* (1 Kings 18:21)

Moses also spoke plainly to the children of Israel saying; *"I call heaven and earth to record this day against you, that I have set before you life and death, blessing and cursing; therefore choose life that both thou and thy seed shall live."* (Deuteronomy 30:19)

Joshua commanded the children of Israel to, *"choose this day whom you will serve, but as for me and my house, we will serve the Lord."* (Joshua 24:15)

Orpah had reached her own turning point in life and having kissed her mother in law and Ruth goodbye, off she went to her own people and her hometown.

Contrastingly, Ruth had reached a similar turning point but somehow managed to do the opposite of her sister in law by embracing the idea of a new country and culture and so clung to Naomi with incredible loyalty and immense hope. Even the strongest and most passionate protests of Naomi, *"Your sister-in-law is going back to her people and her gods. Go back with her"*, fell on deaf ears.

Ruth refused to bend. She was made of different stuff and knew Naomi had lost everything and couldn't cope alone. Unlike Orpah, Ruth preferred to let the dead bury their dead, setting her face towards life and Bethlehem.

Sure she would have been apprehensive, but unlike her ambitionless sister, she was willing to get out of her comfort zone and go after her dream.

Are you Ruth or Orpah?

There's a cost in going after our dreams. Ruth would go

from being known and respected in Moab, to unknown and even second class in Bethlehem. Ruth had made it in Moab, but in Bethlehem she would have to begin all over again, which was no mean feat!

But the desire to follow her dream and stand by her broken mother-in-law meant she was determined to press on.

As Naomi pressed on, her loyal daughter-in-law sprinted after her and fell at her feet, a symbol of total submission. With floods of tears she made one last plea to her mother in law uttering a classic statement of devotion and legendary biblical text;*"Entreat me not to leave thee, or to return from following after thee; for whither thou goest, I will go; and where thou lodgest, I will lodge; thy people shall be my people; and thy God my God."* (Ruth 1:16 KJV)

Ruth's grand announcement of allegiance is a choice to embrace the God who had, apparently, so decisively rejected Naomi, and therefore Ruth refuses to add to her distress by dismissing her.

"Please allow me to accompany you to Bethlehem," cried an inconsolable Ruth, but Naomi continued to fight the idea fiercely.

"Listen to me, Ruth, life in Israel is so different to Moab, our laws and ways won't suit you. The reality is you couldn't cope there, and anyway, Orpah needs you. Quickly, if you hurry you can catch her because she has far heavier bags than you."

"You need me more, Mother. You don't get it, I want to go wherever you go, I want to live where you live."

"How many times do I need to explain, Ruth? Our

people are different, and the culture is opposite to the culture you have known. Besides I am a bitter woman because the Lord has brought such suffering upon me."

The tears began to flow from Ruth's eyes, her heart breaking she refused to give in.

"I don't care; I will help you heal, Mother. Your people will become my people and better still; your God will become my God. Where you die, I want to die, and wherever you get buried I wish to be buried. Only death will separate you and me now."

Naomi gasped at the depth of Ruth's devotion and love. It warmed her heart. It wasn't the same feeling of love she remembered with Elimelech and her two sons, but it filled a void and an ache she never imagined possible. Maybe she should accept this gift of love as being from the Lord Himself.

"Oh, Ruth, I am so blessed to have a daughter like you. You truly are special and a blessing and comfort from God."

"I am the blessed one, Mother." Ruth replied, modestly playing down her outstanding attributes of love and loyalty.

Ruth had made a conscious decision to leave the gods of Moab in exchange for the God of Israel; she had accepted the God of Abraham, Isaac, and Jacob; the true and living God, she had accepted Jehovah, in place of the dead and ancient gods of Moab.

She found hope in Naomi's faith and had now come to rely on Naomi's God.

When Naomi took her step toward God, it was natural for Ruth to pursue her. She had chosen the grace of God over the way of the flesh.

Contrastingly, Orpah, who, for all her life, had hoped in the flesh, was destined to return to the idols with which she was familiar. She was sure to return to her people and natural lifestyle.

Not so Ruth! She is a picture of those today who will choose to serve and follow God regardless of the hardship involved.

The Bible outlines how in the last days which you and I live, some, like Ruth, will willingly accept the message of the gospel and receive the grace of God, choosing to follow the leading of the Spirit, while others like Orpah will reject it and choose death.

Think about it! These girls lived together but chose entirely different paths.

One remained faithful to Israel and its God, the other to Moab.

All along, two hearts had been living under one roof but two very different souls and life choices!

Ruth chose gain; Orpah chose loss. Ruth opted for peace and prosperity, Orpah elected for fear and poverty.

Speaking of His Second Coming, Jesus talked about how, *"two would be in a field, and one would be taken and the other left."* (Mathew 24:40)

Naomi, Orpah and Ruth are a representation of us all reaching a moment of crucial decision in our lives.

Naomi returned to her roots, Ruth left her roots, while Orpah went back to her roots.

In the story of Abraham, he had a nephew named Lot, a man who was an image of the flesh. God wanted to bless Abraham, but God couldn't give a blessing to him because of Lot who continually desired what was pleasant to the flesh. Abraham wanted to remain with Lot because he loved him and, after all, Lot was his nephew. But when they left Egypt, both wealthy, there were quarrels because the heart of Lot was different from the heart of Abraham. While Lot didn't quarrel with Abraham directly, his herdsmen began to disagree with the herdsmen of Abraham. That was the evidence that there were complaints against Abraham in the heart of Lot. The Bible says Abraham, without hesitation, told Lot to leave him. *"If thou wilt take the left hand, then I will go to the right; or if thou depart to the right hand, then I will go to the left."* (Genesis 13:9)

It was akin to saying, "I cannot walk with you."

Abraham had discovered that he could not walk with Lot anymore and decided to send Lot away from him.

In her heart, neither could Orpah walk a single step further with Naomi because Orpah's heart had not received the Lord.

And, so, the Lord said to Abraham, after Lot left him, *"where thou art, northward, and southward and eastward, and westward. For all the land which thou seest to thee will I give it, and to thy seed forever. And I will make thy seed as the dust of the earth; so that if a man can number the dust of the earth; then thy seed also be numbered. Arise; walk through this land in the length of it and the breadth of it; for I will give it unto thee."* (Genesis 13:14-17)

Thereafter, Abraham's blessings increased once Lot left him. Similarly, when Naomi was in Moab, she wasn't blessed. Both cruelty and tragedy had visited her, but when Orpah returned home, (the last remembrance of Moab) Naomi stepped out in faith trusting God and her blessing was awaiting her in Bethlehem. Having left Moab behind, Ruth followed her, and the grace of God was just around the corner for both. Of course, after everything they'd been through; it took great faith on behalf of both Naomi and Ruth to get up and go to Bethlehem, but they were single-minded women with immense faith, determined to test God's will for their lives.

As they journeyed on, Naomi sought to comfort her courageous daughter-in-law. "Don't worry, Ruth, God will provide for us, and He will not disappoint us. God is faithful, and when we walk in His ways and His will, he hears us and delivers us from every trial."

That was more like the old Naomi. Even though Naomi was carrying considerable bitterness following her experiences in Moab, Ruth recognised a returning faith in her mother-in-law which brought reassurance. She recalled how Naomi had spoken so positively in Moab before the awful tragedies they all had endured and perhaps now that positivity could return.

Nevertheless, as they slept under the stars, and due to enter Bethlehem the next day, Ruth began to consider her future and just what her new life would be like.

She must have experienced the same emotions Naomi went through when she first set out for Moab all those years before. Fear and apprehension far outweighed any excitement. Ruth had made grand promises and vows, but talk is cheap!

Could she eventually honour them? Only time would tell. Then she began to pray inwardly, a sign that Ruth had not only decided to follow Naomi to Bethlehem but also her God.

"Oh, Lord, strengthen me and help me and make me a blessing to this wonderful lady Naomi. Direct our paths and keep us both safe in your tender care. Lead us to the right people, people who will help us and bless us and take care of us initially as we settle in Israel. And teach me your ways and show me the things of God, those amazing things Naomi has talked to me about for so many years."

Naomi was also fearful, and, like Ruth, had many questions such as how would her family, friends, and brethren receive her?

Would she get a warm welcome in Bethlehem or encounter rejection?

Would there be dirty looks, harsh stares, and the cold shoulder?

It was a worrying prospect for both Naomi and Ruth. She'd been away for many years and had experienced enough rejection in Moab to last a lifetime.

How would the natives feel about her returning with a foreign daughter-in-law?

Would she be viewed as an outcast, someone cursed and even unclean?

But, what had she got to lose? For her, Moab was history.

Dead and buried!

Only Bethlehem, the town of her birth and Israel, held any lasting promise and potential. To return there was a considerable risk, but a risk she simply knew she had to take.

Nine

There's no place like home

So they two went until they came to Bethlehem. And it came to pass when they were come to Bethlehem, that all the city was moved about them, and they said, Is this Naomi?

And she said unto them, Call me not Naomi, call me Mara: for the Almighty hath dealt very bitterly with me. I went out full and the Lord hath brought me home again empty: why then call ye me Naomi, seeing the Lord hath testified against me, and the Almighty hath afflicted me?

So Naomi returned, and Ruth the Moabitess, her daughter in law, with her, which returned out of the country of Moab: and they came to Bethlehem at the beginning of barley harvest. (Ruth 1-19-22)

Staggering through the outskirts of the town, people observed the two strangers as they stumbled into Bethlehem.

Penniless, their fortunes lost, the pair approached their new quarters with apprehension.

Bethlehem was so lush and bountiful in comparison to Moab. It had altered from the destitution Naomi recalled and experienced all those years ago. There was a different feel to the place; it was a more prosperous and healthy community.

The locals were smiling, and better times were evident. Strength had returned and with it a spiritual awakening.

Nothing improves the lives of people and nations like the blessing of God.

Solomon wrote; *"Righteousness exalts a nation, but sin is a reproach to any people."* (Proverbs 14:34)

The English Standard Version reads; *"Godliness makes a nation great, but sin is a disgrace to any people."*

Israel was again prospering due to the blessing of the Lord! With many nations in trouble today, the hope for our world is not necessarily better government or more intelligence. Many times, we blame the government for the dreadful state of affairs, but people usually get the government and the outcome they deserve.

The economy is not our highest priority, either, righteousness is!

The revival of nations is still possible when people pursue God. And when God decides to bless a country, as He did with Israel, we can only celebrate how true blessings are from heaven's throne and appreciate all the more how every good gift comes from the Father above.

Solomon reminds us why numerous nations are currently impoverished and without the blessing of the Lord stating; *"When the righteous are in authority the people rejoice, but when the wicked bear rule, the people mourn."* (Proverbs 29:2)

During the days of Elimelech, everyone had done that which was right in their own eyes, the wicked were in control, and many suffered the consequences of their disobedience.

Even Elimelech, whose name means "My God is King" ignored his King and sadly perished along with his sons.

What changed in Israel during the years which followed? Probably a structure of God's government was in place, and the people had made peace with God.

This new atmosphere in Israel allowed Naomi to find a way to return to the land of her birth. She was finally able to go home! Forced to live abroad, Naomi had missed her home, and the joy of returning must have been extraordinary.

After all, home is where the heart is!

The first generation to settle on the moon were ecstatic with their remarkable accomplishment, but the earth was home and where their hearts were.

Five hours after blasting off from the Kennedy Space Centre in Florida on December 7, 1972, an astronaut took a picture which showed the earth in all its spherical glory.

The Blue Marble is still NASA's most requested picture. As they disappeared into the blackness of space and caught the last sight of earth, someone is alleged to have said; "There's no place like home."

Home is a place where everything is familiar. Why do many of us long for our homeland when, like Naomi, we choose or are forced to live elsewhere?

Extensive research provides the answer. It suggests there's no place like home because humans construct the image of our last days in memory and imagination. Our desire to remain tied to a specific place relates to burying our dead. "Home is where the heart is" simply means: our hearts are often with our loved ones, brethren and friends and where we will end our lives. Home is a representation of cultural identity and thus provides a collective sense of social permanency and security. It is where the term "homesickness" originates.

Homesickness, of course, can be quite distressing and due to the pain of separation from those we care for it can make many people miserable. Even believers are known to yearn for, their spiritual home when forced to work, worship or live elsewhere.

It was the condition of Naomi before her return to Bethlehem.

In Moab, her desire for her homeland had become so intense she had grown tired and discouraged, and sad and empty in her spirit. And so, no obstacle and no fear would ultimately prevent her from returning to a country she loved with all her heart.

No obstacle could prevent her from resettling in the land of her birth.

With Elimelech out of the picture, Naomi could no longer stick sitting in Moab surrounded by bad memories, while her people tried to revive their nation. She had a duty to return and be part of such a revival. Having learned that there was bread again in Israel she longed to make up for the years she'd gone missing.

Many believers and even biblical greats have known the pain of having to live in a foreign country away from their culture of birth. The great Nehemiah, who returned from Babylon to help rebuild the broken walls of Jerusalem, was a man who became miserable and sad during his exile in a foreign land. He, too, had become despondent away from the city of Jerusalem. His depressing disposition even caused the King to ask, *"Why does your face look so sad?"* (Nehemiah 2:2)

Nehemiah was sad because he'd been away from Judah and Jerusalem for far too long. He desperately missed his brethren, culture and religion — and so it was time to return. It wasn't only homesickness that inspired Nehemiah to return, however. His answer to the King regarding his sadness of heart shows another motive behind Nehemiah's desire to come home — the desire to see his brethren and nation restored.

Nehemiah stated; *"Why should my face not look sad when the city where my ancestors are buried lies in ruins and the gates are burned with fire?"* (Nehemiah 3:3)

Like Naomi, Nehemiah was an Israelite who loved his people, church, brethren and culture. It grieved him greatly to hear of their struggles and especially when he had the heart to help his brethren and his nation recover.

Essentially he said; *"If my brethren are struggling I want to help out. If the church is weak, I must return and make it strong again. If my country is under siege, I want to be there to defend it."*

I'm sure many in Babylon didn't understand Nehemiah's desire to return to such a place, especially given his privileged position in Babylon as the King's Cupbearer. After all, who would trade such a comfortable state of affairs for a land in trouble? But people rarely see the inner motives of our hearts when they are pure.

Permit me to ask: How much do we truly love our brethren, our home church, the community we live in and our nation of birth?

If our brethren are struggling will we go to help them?

If our church is weak will we stay until it is strong again, rather than project apathy during its downfall or disappear during its greatest time of need?

If our country is under attack will we defend its cause and remain true to its Christian ethos?

Home is not just where the heart is; it's often a sign that we are in the right place.

We are always at home in the will of God and Naomi more than most had come to understand this truth.

Nehemiah also knew that until he was home, back in the centre of God's will, there would be no joy in his heart and no blessing in his life. The material conditions may not have proved as prosperous as Babylon, but Nehemiah was more interested in the prosperity of his soul and the souls of his brethren than his flesh.

Naomi, too, had left the wicked and the cursed surroundings of Moab for the righteous and blessed streets of Bethlehem and she'd brought Ruth with her.

In her case, the conditions were now even better than Moab. Wheat was in abundance, just like the 'good old days' but another question beckoned: could these two wandering women produce a plentiful supply for themselves?

Here was a crucial issue!

By God's grace, Israel was prospering again, but not Moab, and not Naomi or Ruth.

They were two immigrants who had absolutely nothing.

It takes great courage to move to another culture; in fact, in most cases, it's a death-defying feat so why do people risk everything in this way? The answer is frequently for the expectation of a better life, and this was the hope of Naomi, but it doesn't always prove fruitful.

Elimelech, for example, had risked all by leaving Israel yet instead he found and experienced the thing he was trying to avoid — disappointment and death. Perhaps there's no better time to study the story of Naomi and her family in light of what is taking place around our world today. Cultural change and the refugee crisis are reshaping our society, yet it is certainly nothing new. Immigration is full of pitfalls and danger, but beautiful things can still emerge. In the midst of their trials, both Naomi and Ruth, two immigrants, forged an unbreakable interracial relationship and how topical is that?

Naomi had left a barren and unfruitful field in search of the blessing of God, knowing all too well that there were only four ways she could possibly survive.

Firstly, she and Ruth would have to work in another man's field gathering the left over's, but this was seemingly impossible as Naomi was too old to work and Ruth being a foreigner from the land of Moab would have been hated and scorned. An outcast, her life would be in danger every day in those fields.

Secondly, Naomi could marry, but again she felt beyond marriage due to the passing years.

Thirdly, her children could support her, but she had lost her children who were all dead.

And fourthly, she could rent her land, but the ground was gone too, and the name of Elimelech had become extinct.

To say Naomi and Ruth were economically bankrupt and caught between a rock and a hard place is no exaggeration having been left bereft of everything which gave meaning in society?

Naomi had one thing in her favour, however, like Joseph, the Lord was with her guiding her steps wherever she went. She had a deep faith in God, all-be-it, that same faith had taken quite a battering. And despite the passing of time, she was still recognisable and striking. Naomi wasn't just spiritual, she was beautiful and unforgettable, even in her later years.

One look at her stunning complexion could warm the coldest of hearts. Beauty was Naomi's middle name and so it was only a matter of time before her arrival in Bethlehem became headline news. The Bible describes her and Ruth's entrance thus; *"So they two went until they came to Bethlehem. And it came to pass when they were come to Bethlehem, that all the city was moved about them, and they said, Is this Naomi?"*

"Naomi, is it you?" said one of her oldest friends.

"I don't believe it; it is you! My dearest friend, you have come back!"

Naomi forced a smile. "Meet Ruth, my daughter."

Her former acquaintance could hardly contain her joy. "This is such an awesome answer to prayer, Naomi. You will never know how much we have prayed for your safe return and how we welcome you to your homeland again."

Having feared rejection, those early words of affirmation were music to Naomi's ears. They confirmed what her friend Avi had told her back in Moab that she was loved, revered, and deeply missed by her people. She wasn't sure whether or not he was saying such a thing merely to comfort and encourage her, but now she began to believe it was true.

She had longed to hear those words of affirmation, and so she and Ruth appeared to be off to a great start. They all kissed and embraced as family members do before being offered a hearty meal.

"You both look so hungry, why not come to our home for something to eat?" said her friend.

It was an offer Naomi and Ruth couldn't refuse. After all, they were tired and starving and in need of food.

As they walked and talked together, stopping to pick up some other supplies in the town, memories flooded back of better days; days when Naomi and Elimelech were first married. Back then all was well with the world. Now things felt scary and unpredictable. It was the same people alright, the same town, but a different era and situation. The streets looked just the same;

even the little fountain where Naomi and Elimelech had first courted remained, although it seemed quite grown over. She recalled how they'd spent many times hugging and kissing there, a time when youthful innocence flourished.

Of course, much water had passed under the bridge since then, but she could recall those days as if it was yesterday.

There were plenty of familiar faces in the town, but noticeably others seemed to be absent. Had they died off or just quietly left like Naomi and Elimelech during the famine? As they approached the centre of the town, the first thing Naomi had looked for was the sight of the old man keeping watch over the temple. He was always there, day and night, immaculately dressed and ready to give the Word of the Lord when required, yet he, too, seemed to be missing, and the temple itself looked run down and neglected.

"How are things at church?" Naomi asked.

"Don't even go there," replied her friend.

"It has changed since you left, my dear. The people are lukewarm, and the leaders are more interested in their positions than the flock God has given them. But the famine has ended so maybe things will improve spiritually for all of us as well as materially. I feel sorry for the people, the famine has affected us all, but maybe you can encourage them privately Naomi. I always remember how you possessed such a great gift of encouragement."

Naomi had come home to do just that, but in reality, she was a broken woman herself. How do you encourage others when you can't even support yourself? How do you lift up another when you are also on the floor?

Over dinner, they recalled better times which should have produced laughter, yet perhaps unsurprisingly it brought only tears of sorrow for Naomi.

"How we have missed you, Naomi; it's going to be like old times, I know it," insisted her friend.

Naomi remained motionless. Having been absent for so long, and through so much, it was always going to be a difficult step to return to her roots, but all of a sudden, the enormity of such a prospect was hitting home. No one in Bethlehem could have understood even half of what she had been through in Moab. Aware of the fact that she'd lost everything, seeing the people of Bethlehem prosper again only seemed to compound the situation. She was glad they were recovering from the famine, but she also began to compare what she'd lost to what many who had remained had gained.

"If only we had stayed put" was a sentence which came flooding back to her mind and heart time and again.

"If only we'd toughed it out, we might all still be together."

"Eat some bread and take something to drink, Naomi?" urged her friend, who by now noticed the concern in Naomi's weary face.

Then, without warning, poor Naomi couldn't contain her emotions any longer revealing the anger inside her. "Please, please, stop it, don't call me Naomi."

Awkward stares took place until she finally broke the silence.

"Don't ever call me Naomi again or 'pleasant' either because I am a long way from being pleasant. I may have gone out full, but I have returned empty. Can't you see we've lost everything?

Another silence and embarrassment followed, but relief was present, too. After all, Naomi had finally exploded, told the truth and got things out in the open. Every step of that journey from Moab she had bottled up thoughts about the past until she became overflowing with recriminations.

"I have a new name now which is Mara meaning bitterness and emptiness; it sums up everything about me."

The book of Ruth recites it this way; *"So they two went until they came to Bethlehem. And it came to pass when they were come to Bethlehem, that all the city was moved about them, and they said, is this Naomi? And she said unto them, Call me not Naomi, call me Mara: for the Almighty hath dealt very bitterly with me. I went out full and the Lord hath brought me home again empty: why then call ye me Naomi, seeing the Lord hath testified against me, and the Almighty hath afflicted me?"* (Ruth 1:19-21)

In the same way, God was not against Jacob, even though Jacob had convinced himself everything was against him, neither was God the enemy of Naomi. Nor had He afflicted her, because God always had her best interests at heart. Most of her pain and suffering was merely the result of wrong decision making on the part of her husband.

So often we blame God for calamities we brought on ourselves, and Naomi was no different.

Her friend quickly responded. "We heard all about your setbacks my companion. It's a small world, Naomi. No one wanted this for you. But remember, people, begged you not to leave. Our brethren pleaded with Elimelech not to go to Moab. If only you had stayed here none of that dreadful stuff would have happened to you and your family?"

"My duty is first to the Lord and then to Elimelech. I had no choice but to go with my husband. Don't you think I'm aware of how costly our decision has proved?"

Naomi, more than anyone, had already learned the hard way. She didn't need to hear "I told you so." She didn't require a rebuke or further recrimination. What she needed was love and acceptance and hope for the future and faith to believe in life, love and most of all in God and her people again.

Here is evidence of genuine Christian character and the pure love of God in our hearts — the desire to see people restored, not condemned for the unfortunate decisions they make.

The reality is all of us have made poor decisions at crucial times in our lives.

Pointing out someone's failures is never as useful as reminding them of their successes and God-given potential.

We've all failed and messed up in some way. People who have fallen must be helped up again, and principally by the church. Paul wrote; *"Brethren, if a man is caught in any transgression, you who are spiritual should restore such a one in the spirit of meekness, watching yourselves, lest you also be tempted."* (Galatians 6:1-2)

The key word in this text is the word "spiritual." Only spiritual people with the grace of God in their lives are truly equipped to restore others properly. Religious people and teachers of the law cannot restore others, because they do not understand grace or forgiveness. They may talk about God and even present God in some plausible manner, but God is far from their hearts.

Naomi may not have failed or messed up in her service to God, but through the choices, she and her family made, it was evident to all that her circumstances had deteriorated drastically. She had become bereft and impoverished. She was a child of God in significant need of assistance.

It left her friend and sister in the Lord with only two choices — to remind her of her past or assist her to reach the next phase of her life; to offer her positivity or negativity.

Helping others to achieve the next stage of their journey following any form of catastrophe or setback is a noble goal for every church minister and professing Christian. Here is the clear evidence of the grace of God.

How much more attractive is a church which not only preaches the message of restoration, but also practices it?

Jesus rebuked the Pharisees for ignoring those who had fallen and those who are spiritually weak stating; *"They that be whole need, not a physician, but they that are sick."* (Matthew 9:22)

It is beautiful to meet people with Christ in their hearts rather than those with moral standards in their heads. Imagine going home to your family having experienced considerable distress only to be told by them you are a failure and no longer welcome? When the Prodigal Son returned having wasted his inheritance, the Bible says that the Father was waiting for him ready to restore him and hold a party of hope for him. The father put a ring on his finger and a robe on him.

On the other hand, the elder brother became angry, and refused to go to the party celebrating his brother's return.

He possessed an unforgiving spirit of jealousy and anger.

When the apostle Peter denied the Lord Jesus before his crucifixion, less than forty days later Jesus asked the disciples to bring Peter with them and meet him in Galilee.

Why?

To reinstate and restore him in the purpose of God for his life.

God is a restoring God!

And no one needed to be restored and given hope more than Naomi. The joy she once radiated which made her "beautiful" and "pleasant", was all gone.

Her darkened countenance and sad eyes told a story of immense sorrow and suffering and painted a picture of a life destroyed, but not a life without hope. Where God is there is always hope!

She was home, but she came home battered and bruised. With the help of her people and a loving and merciful God, she required much love and acceptance, constant words of affirmation, love and support, not criticism and hostility.

Feeling empty and bitter Naomi needed a miracle, and was about to get one, but not in a way she would ever have expected.

Ten

The Right Place at the Right Time

"And she went and came, and gleaned in the field after the reapers; and her hap was to light on the part of the field belonging unto Boaz, who was of the kindred of Elimelech."
(Ruth 2:3)

Restoration takes time, but it's always worth the wait. Everything happens in God's timing, and every new move and fresh anointing comes with a sweet sound. That fresh anointing and different resonance were about to emerge in the life of Naomi; her suffering was nearing completion; her time of darkness was getting replaced by great light and new hope. Weeping had endured for a night, but great joy was coming in the morning!

Of course, neither Naomi nor Ruth was aware of this joy and welcome change, only of the obvious difference in the environment they'd come to. It may have been a more prosperous Bethlehem than the one Naomi had left behind all those years ago, but both her and Ruth still required necessary living provisions such as food and water. Survival was key!

Having arrived in Bethlehem, Naomi sensed a surreal feeling of finally being home and once this reality set in, the only thing she could do was gasp a sigh of relief and cry out; *"Thank you, Lord, for your mercy and a new start."*

But where would both women reside? With no provision and not exactly welcome, due mainly to Ruth's background, they were technically homeless. Two children of God, who'd become refugees, sleeping under the stars in the same way that many poor souls continue to sleep under the stars today, camped in doorways and left to lie under bridges and on the streets?

We may currently live in the 21st century, technology and knowledge have undoubtedly increased, but homelessness is nothing new and continues to blight our modern-day cities and countries. Even Jesus, a King and our Saviour understood the pain of having to live without a roof over His head. The book of Luke declares; *"Foxes have holes, and the birds of the air have nests, but the Son of man has nowhere to lay his head."* (Luke 9:58)

It seems hard to fathom that Jesus, King of Kings and Lord of Lords, spent many nights under the stars and here, too, was the plight of these two brave women, Ruth and Naomi; back in Bethlehem, but homeless and needy. Back in the will of God, but not back to any form of security or normality. As they bedded down for the night, probably in a cave, Naomi did what most of us would do in a similar situation — she prayed for God's hand of favour for them both and His mercy. In those days, many wanderers used caves as shelter from the storms of life, in particular the caves not presently occupied.

When you are as tired and discouraged as these two women, beggars cannot be choosers. It's a relief to rest anywhere. Even a cave feels like home if it is somewhere to lay your hat. They didn't have much, just each other and God, but strange as it seems, this is the place where the Almighty begins to work in our lives — the site of emptiness and lack.

The following day promised little, but it would be the beginning of a miraculous season in their lives and the commencement of an astonishing period of restoration. God would not disappoint either Naomi or Ruth.

They'd arrived in Bethlehem bereft at the beginning of the barley season (late April/early May); shortly after which would follow the wheat harvest. Perfect timing for two widows needing food, as gleaning laws in Israel required landowners to leave corners of fields and all fallen shafts of grain for the poor. How great a consolation this would have been to both Naomi and Ruth? Suddenly the future looked bright again. Help was at hand and survival possible. A change of fortune was in the wind. Never underestimate the power of tomorrow and God's ability to restore what has been lost.

Our lack doesn't limit God. He never disappoints. He can bring grace and blessings out of the worst despair. His goodness always exceeds our expectations, and His timing is perfect. There are no accidents with Him; *"The steps of a good man are ordered of the Lord, and he delights in his way."* (Psalm 37:23)

Naomi and Ruth were both faithful women and God had acknowledged their faithfulness and directed their paths. What seemed like a random place to work proved to be no fluke. Here instead was evidence of the guidance of a merciful God in the lives of these two forlorn travellers.

In the same way, God had led Abraham's servant to the house where Rebekah lived (Genesis:4), so He had now taken the steps of Naomi and Ruth to the field of their future provision and redeemer. Whatever situation you are currently in, whatever difficult point you are at, it is only ever for a season. God will eventually direct your steps away from poverty, persecution and struggle. The words of Jeremiah reveal how God's ultimate plan and purpose for our lives is restoration; *"For I know the thoughts that I think towards you, saith the Lord, thoughts of peace and not of evil, to give you an expected end."* (Jeremiah 29:11)

Though these two women had previously believed themselves to be alone, it soon transpired this wasn't the case. Not only was God by their side, they had a relative, who just happened to be a man of standing and great influence in Bethlehem.

God, in His great mercy, had a supernatural and blessed end planned for both Naomi and Ruth and it included this wealthy relative of Naomi's by the name of Boaz.

Just as the darkness of night is replaced with the break of dawn, a new day of hope had beckoned. Ruth appeared to embrace and perceive this new position much quicker than her mother-in-law.

"It's time, Mother; I am going to visit the fields to glean."

The statement shocked Naomi. "I can't allow you, it's my role, and I won't let you go there."

"I disagree; your place is in the home, Mother; please permit me to do this for you."

"It's too dangerous for you, Ruth. You will need me to accompany you."

"I'm not a baby. Why are you so protective of me?"

"Why? I'm almost ashamed to admit it, Ruth, but there are people in my country who have no time for foreigners. They can be so nasty and so lacking in mercy and consideration for poor people also."

"I thought you said Israel was a godly nation, Mother?"

"It's a great nation, Ruth, but many of my people are still unwilling to love their neighbour as they have been commanded to do."

"Every country produces people like that. Trust me; I can look after myself. I will be fine. I'd prefer you to stay home and relax and even pray to God for us today."

There seems to have been a cultural acceptance that in, those days, women gleaning in the fields were vulnerable, especially foreign women, hence Naomi's concern. But sensing how determined Ruth was, Naomi soon relented. Remember, she'd lost the battle to make Ruth return to her homeland and was no match for her loyal and devoted daughter in law in this struggle either. Ruth was a feisty, strong female.

"Fine, but promise me you'll take care, I mean it, Ruth, those fields can be dangerous for foreign girls like you. Some men will see you as an easy target."

"I'll be fine, Mother. Tell you what, I will work, and you can pray and let's see what the God of Israel does."

"Oh, Ruth, you are maturing so quickly in your faith and remind me of how I used to be before the cold winds of adversity polluted my spirit. To hear such uninhibited and pure faith in God has refreshed my spirit this day."

"You will bounce back and soon, Mother, and don't underestimate yourself; I can still recognise God's hand upon your life, too. I know you say not to call you pleasant anymore, but I can still see many traces of pleasantness in you. It's more than a name meaning, its part of your personality, mother."

Having eased Naomi's fears, the two embraced and parted, leaving Naomi to slip back inside their temporary cave. She sat down, took a deep breath and wondered how they'd made it this far. Close to her chest, she clutched garments belonging to Elimelech, Mahlon, and Chilion, garments she'd kept for years. It was all she had left of them, yet the time had come to put them away for good. She would never forget her beloved husband and sons, but Naomi began to understand that no one can live in the present and arrive in the future if they continuously live in the past.

Along with other relics, she folded them up one last time and placed them in a bag which never got opened again from that day forward. It was a painful moment which brought grief and sorrow to her heart, but also a moment which needed tackled to bring closure. She couldn't avoid it any longer.

And so, reverting to tried and tested methods; she began to do what had always worked before, and what Ruth had suggested earlier; Naomi, that great woman of God, finally started to return to the place of prayer.

Powerfully and sincerely, she prayed God would heal her heart and, of course, Ruth's and Orpah's. She hadn't forgotten poor little Orpah. She thought about her every day and repented of every stupid act before, during and even after their Moab ordeal. She forgave her husband and herself for the decisions they'd made and began calling on God again to open "new doors," if not for her sake, at least for Ruth's. Moving on would require honesty and repentance and Naomi managed to summon both.

"God, please hear and respond to our cry and send help from your people. Do what seems impossible to Ruth and me and restore to me everything that the enemy has taken."

Remarkably, as Naomi spoke with her God, He was already answering her prayer. Like Daniel, who from the first time he cried out, the response was on the way, so, too, Naomi's cries reached heaven's throne and just as Ruth's miracle was about to unfold. Notwithstanding; Ruth's initial arrival at the barley fields was still met with serious hostility. Recognising she was a foreigner, gleaners hurled insults and items at Ruth which saw her quickly flee. Maybe Naomi was right; perhaps she should have remained at home, after all?

> "Clear off! Moabites are not welcome. We are sick of people like you coming over here and taking our jobs and food. Go home, you useless beggar. We've no time here for foreigners like you."

Thousands of years may have passed since, yet history is repeating itself.

In the same callous way Ruth was made unwelcome, many refugees and immigrants today endure similar malice, hatred, and prejudice when arriving to find work in a strange land. Foreigners being hounded out of their properties and told to go back to where they came from, due to fear that they will 'take jobs,' 'gain power' and 'take over,' is now commonplace in many countries. The same racism and intolerance that existed in Ruth and Naomi's generation are sadly alive and well in the 21st century and in most cases, even worse. It's become a global problem having now subverted many other countries.

How do God and the land of Israel view hostility such as this?

Here is a crucial question for God's people and the church in our present age. God has always desired that we "reach out" to people of all faiths and backgrounds with the good news of the gospel, not reject them.

The love of God is much bigger, broader and higher than the confines of one skin colour, one church, one faith and one theological viewpoint. God is a welcoming God to all who will receive Him. The book of John records; *"God so loved the world that He gave His only begotten Son that whosoever believes in Him shall not perish but shall have everlasting life."* (John 3:16)

Herein are the real heart and nature of our Creator. If God receives people from every background, then why would His children reject them?

As Ruth shrugged off those preliminary insults and progressed to another field, searching desperately for a greeting from some friendly face, a worker approached her and offered her a kind and welcome smile.

"You are new here, right?"

Ruth smiled and nodded.

"Don't worry you will get the hang of it. Its hard work, but anyone can do it."

"My name is Ruth; I am the daughter of Naomi."

"Nice to meet you, Ruth. I'm Mr. Labourer."

Ruth laughed. "Nice to meet you, too, Mr. Labourer."

Mr Labourer's kind words must have proved welcome to an immigrant like Ruth, stranded in another country and different culture to the one she grew up in and not knowing a single soul. How grateful she must have been for this one smiling face and friendly individual.

His gesture of goodwill is the evidence of the kindness of God towards the outsider and less fortunate. Ruth, of course, was a "poor foreigner," but the Israelite in the field still welcomed her with open arms. She was nervous, and frightened, not knowing what to do on her first day in her new country, yet she received a friendly welcome. It settled her and gave her hope.

I wonder do we welcome foreigners in the same way to our own countries especially in light of the mass migration which has taken place globally.

Do we welcome them with open arms like Mr. Labourer and with a friendly disposition or hurl insults at them and tell them to "get lost" and to "go back home?"

Today foreigners and migrants already exist under increasing dark clouds of suspicion in many Western countries. Media reports the arrival of asylum-seekers in "waves" that threaten to "swamp" our shores — in fact, the influx of vulnerable migrants described as a threatening natural disaster has become common.

A biblical response to asylum-seeking is, therefore, essential.

While not every immigrant wants to be "redeemed," refugees are also crucial to our well-being especially in relation to employment. Many have proved a blessing to different countries in numerous ways.

Notwithstanding; when it comes to the matter of Salvation, God redeems who He pleases and finds a way to channel His "covenant love," regardless of status or bloodline or standard of living, He takes great delight in bringing the refugee like Ruth, the foreigner and the stranger from outside to the inside of His covenant.

The Bible is full of accounts of how God can reach the seemingly unreachable.

In the Old Testament, both Tamar and Rahab were harlots who found redemption. Ruth was a heathen and Bathsheba an adulterous woman. In the New Testament, a Samaritan woman at a well who had many husbands also experienced the saving grace of God following a life-changing encounter with Jesus.

We can only but marvel at the nature of God's mercy for people such as Tamar, Rahab, Ruth and Bathsheba, the woman at the well and the expansive reach of His love towards His entire creation. Why then are many Christians seemingly prepared to reject the struggling stranger rather than reaching out to these poor souls with the grace of a loving and compassionate God?

Like Ruth; it takes great courage to move to another country and culture and yet millions of refugees are on the move in such a manner today. The 21st century story of Doaa Al Zamel is just one account of the harrowing experiences millions of refugees today go through. She was one of only eleven people to survive after being left floating for four horrible days in the sea. The boat she was travelling on was carrying more than 500 people — many from Syria— but sank near Greece. Doaa Al Zamel miraculously managed to stay afloat while holding on to two babies that were handed to her by their drowning relatives.

Author, Melissa Fleming shares Al Zamel's story in her excellent book *A Hope More Powerful Than the Sea*. It's not just a sad and tragic story, however, but a story that highlights incredible resilience and hope.

If we can show love and care towards the destitute, we will, in turn, become a blessing to all families of the earth, and eliminate the fears that make us unwilling to be the vessels of grace to those who live as strangers among us.

As a result, therefore, how should we treat someone like Ruth, a foreigner from another country? With the same love and acceptance God expected from those in Biblical days! Are you aware that God's intention for foreigners in the life of the nation is inclusive and lavish? For example, in Naomi and Ruth's generation, gleaners picked up left overs which, in today's society, is a picture of the social welfare system. They dropped handfuls on purpose, beautiful blessings on the ground. No one in God's eyes was to be left starving. The story of Ruth outlines and underlines God's provision spiritually as well as His provision materially.

Having served as a missionary for some years, observing countries where there is no such thing as a "benefits system" or "social welfare", I've witnessed at close quarters the dreadful reality of extreme poverty and starvation. If folk couldn't get work, they didn't eat. Instead, they waited on some compassionate soul or missionary person who would drop a parcel of food to their homes or say a kind word to them. Many western countries are blessed to have a robust welfare system, but sadly just as many other countries fail to provide such benevolence.

Here is what sets Israel and the church apart from every other nation and religious establishment — great acts of compassion and kindness and a welcoming spirit due to the love of Almighty God.

Even secular governments have acknowledged that if we remove the enormous contribution of the church to struggling nation's and people groups; the world would be in a considerably worse place. When it comes to poverty and pain, we are indeed our brother's keeper!

"There is no injustice worse than losing one's dignity which comes as a result of poverty," said Nelson Mandela.

Those left over's in the Barely fields at least gave the poor like Ruth and Naomi their dignity and something to hope for and hope is important for every individual from every background in our society.

Solomon wrote; *"Hope deferred makes the heart sick."* (Proverbs 13:12)

Can you imagine Ruth's reaction to the kindness she experienced, having come from a selfish, self-serving, dog-eat-dog, ungodly land like Moab and having arrived with her dignity at rock bottom? Used all her life to a self-regarding society, suddenly she couldn't comprehend why she became favoured, but she just kept picking the stuff up that God was providing.

How this must have spoken to her heart! Ruth had discovered a different way of life and also experienced consideration and compassion and the love of God. No wonder her heart began to turn full circle from the gods of Moab to the God of Naomi! The love of God and His people had not only touched but transformed Ruth's heart.

The world doesn't need a definition of religion; only a demonstration of the love of God and here is what Ruth experienced due to the mercy of God through a humble servant in a field. Despise not the day of small things. The least act of kindness is always stronger than our highest intention. The man in the barley field may have been an ordinary worker, but his friendly nature and kind welcome showed Ruth everything that is good about church and God.

God had directed Ruth to the right place and the right man and at the right time.

Our gifts prosper when we are in the right place, atmosphere, and environment by God's divine design for our lives? That environment doesn't have to look prosperous so long as God is there. He's not intimidated by sad circumstances or poverty-stricken places. On the contrary, it's where He thrives. Ruth and Naomi's restoration began in a field, an empty spot, but that's all God needed to start a revival in their lives.

Of course, the real change of fortune occurred when they decided to swap nation, town, and even culture to prosper. With every step of faith, they took along that path from Moab, they drew closer to their blessing and the right place. They couldn't understand it, but they sensed all along they were getting nearer their breakthrough and this is what drove them on. Their story teaches us several lessons, reminding us especially never to quit! Keep pressing forward! God is taking you closer to His purpose and plan than you imagine. It's not easy to "press" when we are persecuted and impoverished. It's not easy to "press" when we are tired and disappointed but keep pressing anyway. Put the past behind and press toward God's great plan for your life.

The apostle Paul went through unimaginable hindrance and pain, which included shipwrecks, stoning and imprisonment, yet he declared in the book of Philippians; *"This one thing I do, forgetting those things which are behind and reaching forth unto those things which are before, I press toward the mark the prize of the high calling of God in Christ Jesus."* (Philippians 3:13-14)

In the most unlikely way, suddenly Ruth found herself in the right place at the right time. She had no clue as to how it happened. She may have assumed she stumbled upon it, but remember, *"The steps of a good man are ordered of the Lord,"* (Psalm 37:23), and Naomi's God carefully monitored their steps.

From the time Naomi left Israel for Moab until her return to Israel, God was ordering the steps of both women. The book of Ruth states; *"And as she went and came, and gleaned in the field after the reapers; her HAP was to light on the part of the field belonging unto Boaz, who was of the kindred of Elimelech."* (Ruth 2:3)

The word HAP translates as "just happened to" or "stumbled upon". Ruth had just stumbled upon her redeemer and her fortune, but had she? Have you ever stumbled upon the blessing of God and wondered how it happened? Have you ever questioned why you were picked for that job, why strangers were so kind, why provision came just when you thought you wouldn't make it? Why were you delivered from something tragic while others were not? Was this good fortune alone, coincidence or Divine provision and favour?

What caused it to happen?

You were in the right place at the right time!

If things are not working out in your life right now, then perhaps it's time to consider your place. Maybe you need a change of location. Location matters!

It mattered to Abraham, Joseph, Moses, David, and to Naomi and Ruth. Remember how Elimelech removed the blessing from Naomi's life taking her out of the right place? Now she had returned not just to her homeland, but to the will of God for her life where God had quite a surprise in-store. Naomi's God was about to turn the tables and prove that despite our faults and failures, despite our worst impatience and mistakes, God can bring good out of evil. Through their struggles and desperate situations, these lonely widows learned something unchanging and beautiful about God, something all of us eventually come to recognise — God is always on time; He's never too early and He's never too late. He's always in the right place at the right time.

Eleven

Love at First Sight

Then Boaz said to his servant who was in charge of his harvesters, "Whose young woman is this?"
(Ruth 2:5)

Boaz strolled over the brow of the hill and their eyes met. Her hair blowing in the wind, Ruth smiled at him, glanced down and continued her work.

One Smile!

One sparkle from her eyes and Boaz was captivated!

Ruth's extraordinary beauty left him like a love-struck teenager.

Hands on hips and trying to look cool, Boaz approached her.

He was a man used to being in control, yet for the first time in years, he felt utterly out of control. Ruth had blown him away. The stunning girl from Moab had Boaz mesmerised, gazing at her for what seemed like an eternity.

"Can anyone be so exquisite?" he pondered.

"Sir, good news, the crops are prospering, and the future is bright. Is there anything else we can do to improve things?" interrupted one of his servants.

The question fell on deaf ears. Boaz was gone. The wealthy landowner was experiencing something he'd never thought possible, something he'd dreamed of for most of his life, something everyone hopes will happen to them, but never quite believes it will — that beautiful thing called love at first sight.

Not everyone believes in love at first sight, of course, but try telling that to Boaz, a besotted man if ever there was one. His attraction to Ruth was instantaneous. A man of means, this wealthy landowner would have had his pick of the local women, so why this damsel?

What did she have that others didn't?

What spell had she cast over him?

A peasant girl from Moab, much younger than Boaz, she was, of course, desperately in need materially, but remarkably appealing to Boaz who had never truly believed in romantic fate, at least until now.

It wasn't his birthday, but it must have felt like it. Who is this adorable foreigner gleaning in his field? Other women were crouched behind and round about Ruth, but Boaz only had eyes for Ruth. No one else stood a chance! Nothing compared to Ruth. She could have been in a room with a hundred other girls, and Boaz would not have noticed any of them except her.

No one else mattered!

It was a tingling feeling that set his heart on fire; a sensation so warm and so loving, an emotion he hadn't felt before. As Boaz approached the reapers he said, *"The Lord be with you"* and they answered him *"the Lord bless you."*

One of the concerned hired help noticed Boaz, chuckling to himself like a youthful schoolboy.

"Is something wrong, Sir?

"Nothing is wrong, everything is right.Whose young woman is this?" he responded.

"Sorry Sir, we don't normally keep track of the workers so I couldn't tell you who she is. Why are you asking anyway, isn't it obvious she's a foreigner?"

Incensed by the remark Boaz exploded. "Don't ever show your face here again. I will not tolerate that sort of language besides you are indeed supposed to be carefully checking who is coming in and out of this field."

Boaz then began asking others if they knew who Ruth was when; out of nowhere, Mr Labourer approached.

Boaz wasn't generally in the habit of enquiring about young female workers in his field, especially foreign girls. It was inappropriate. He would have been asking for trouble, but in Ruth's case, he threw caution to the wind. As the owner of the entire land, Boaz was a wealthy businessman and had a responsible position. Although he was the prince of the people, he supervised the harvesting of the grain in his barn, to circumvent any immorality or theft both of which were rife in his day. Delighted the famine had passed, Boaz sought rest after having thanked God for bread again in Israel and is believed to have studied the Torah and Jewish law. He was a respected, intelligent and righteous man within his community, known to have a good reputation, for being upright, loyal, and compassionate. His name means "Strength".

Women regularly tried to charm Boaz, telling him how handsome he was but such flattery was evident to him. They wanted him for his position, power and prosperity, not due to love and, he suspected this. He'd become aware of something else, too, his apparent fallibility.

His face was beginning to reveal a few lines. He wasn't getting any younger. If there was such a thing as "true love," then it had escaped him for most of his life. He'd never quite hit it off with anyone. The "perfect someone," was always for "others" and not destined for him.

He'd resigned himself to such a fate long ago and become more and more unhappy and reclusive. He'd thrown himself into his work which was exciting and motivating, but never enough to satisfy his inner dreams and desires. There's more to life than work and ambition. Even Boaz couldn't bury this truth.

The once-aspiring thoughts Boaz coveted of having the perfect family and a happy marriage wouldn't be fulfilled by work alone.

Then he heard the words and reply of Mr Labourer, words which transformed not only his fortunes but the fortunes of both Ruth and Naomi forever, words which would change all of their lives irrevocably.

"She is the young Moabitess woman who came back with Naomi from the land of Moab, Sir. She says her mother-in-law, Naomi, is a relative of yours, the wife of the late Elimelech. The young damsel has been toiling away all day and is a great worker. I have seen this with my own eyes."

The harvester went on to explain how Ruth had asked to be allowed to glean among the bundles behind the farmers.

The word "Harvesters" is a masculine term in Hebrew, and it seems Ruth went to the fields and started work behind the men. When Boaz noticed her, he quickly insisted she remained in the field but beside the women. So intrigued is Boaz he asked, *"To whom does this young girl belong?"* (Ruth 2:5)

A similar question was asked about Ruth's descendant David, in 1 Samuel 17:56-57. After David had slain Goliath Saul enquired *"From whom is this lad?"* Saul's question is less about the identity of David and more a matter of how can boys like David accomplish such a feat. It is unexpected and surprising. Similarly, how come Boaz has seen such kindness and resourcefulness from a Moabite girl?

"Does the young Moabitess have a name?" he further enquired.

"Ruth, I believe."

Ruth.

Someone he'd never met.

Ruth.

From the heathen nation of Moab.

Ruth.

God knows how to shock, and this was no exception!

A woman once regarded in Jewish law as "forbidden fruit"; yet a woman who had followed the God of Naomi and had captured the heart of Boaz in a instant. How had such a feeling crept up on him? Where did it even begin?

Boaz assembled his workers before instructing them to bless Ruth with the blessing of God.

"Allow the young girl form Moab to take grain from the fields without obstruction and leave as many handfuls as possible for her and her mother-in-law, Naomi, who is the wife of our dear brother Elimelech. Anyone who gives this girl a hard time I will personally deal with," commanded a besotted Boaz.

That day had started like any other. Boaz expected to experience what he always experienced, grain, employees, and workers; no one special! Then his eyes spotted the girl from Moab; his heart skipped a beat, and, in a flash, his world turned upside down.

Initially he dreamed she would find a husband in Israel, someone more her age, but a bigger, more farcical dream quickly emerged within him, the thought that he might actually be that husband for Ruth.

Never underestimate what God can do when you least expect it. Never doubt his ability to do the seemingly impossible in an instant. Never question his willingness and influence to answer your most ridiculous prayer.

Boaz and Ruth were from two different worlds; two different cultures, two different generations, yet God had brought them together for just such a time.

The son of Rahab, Boaz was a wealthy landowner of Bethlehem in Judea and kinsman of Elimelech, Naomi's late husband. He would, no doubt, have been exceptionally kind to Ruth because she was a relative of his, yet Boaz perceived her extraordinary beauty and conscientiousness in picking up the grain as she strictly observed the rules prescribed by the law. What grabbed his attention in particular, however, were her grace and her chaste conduct during work which induced Boaz to follow up on who she was.

Boaz knew there is a beauty to be found on the inside, not just on the outside.

Though He was a man of great wealth; Ruth was weak and even more so now having turned her back on her family and having attached herself to the wandering Naomi. She could only dream of the lifestyle and influence enjoyed by Boaz. The hardship Ruth endured and the grief and tragedy she'd suffered had made no impression on her incredible beauty. Her face was still fresh and healthy. With no make-up, professional lights or what we now identify with as "Photoshopped", she was aglow.

Could someone who hadn't spoken a single word to Boaz, suddenly hold the key to his heart?

Could she finally change his life and help fulfil his destiny?

Ruth was so young. Boaz was much older.

Providentially she'd stopped at a spot in the field where the sunlight allowed the beauty of her face to radiate all the more. Her beauty could be seen from her eyes, the doorway to every woman's heart and the place where true love resides. Her eyes were like stars filled with light and love, small and slanted, but a window to her soul.

His strongest fortifications breached, Boaz was now putty in Ruth's hands.

"Hi, I'm, Boaz, you're Ruth, the daughter of Naomi?"

"Yes, sir, it is so," was Ruth's gentle and respectful reply, as she smiled through those same seductive eyes.

"I'm not comfortable with Sir, Boaz will do."

"Yes sir, I mean, yes, Boaz," Ruth had reacted, nervously.

"Listen to me carefully, Ruth. Stay in this field. I have warned the men to leave you alone and allow you to drink water whenever you please from their vessels. You will be safe with the other women."

Not surprisingly, it was a gesture deeply appreciated by Ruth.

"Thank you, so much, Boaz for your incredible kindness."

Naomi had told her to be careful of the men in the field, but suddenly God had removed her fears. God had showered her with blessings and given her great favour. By going to work in the fields, she had taken the first steps of faith, and God had responded with mercy and grace towards her. Amazingly, the landowner, Boaz was protecting her from dangers seen and unseen. She'd arrived with Naomi in Bethlehem hopeless and penniless, but things were looking up. The blessing of the Lord was tenderly tracking her steps. The light was appearing at the end of a very dark tunnel. She couldn't wait to inform Naomi of the exciting developments when she got home, but that would come later for there was still work to complete.

As the sun disappeared for the day, hope sprung eternal inside Ruth's heart, hope she hadn't felt for many days. As they chatted, Boaz remained enchanted. The servants watched as the pair joked and laughed together almost as though they'd known one another all of their lives.

It was a moment Boaz never wanted to end and Ruth, too.

As the smitten landowner left Ruth to continue gleaning

and strutted back up the hill, his servants were concerned about his unusual behaviour with a foreign girl.

"Are you sure you are okay, Sir?"

"Yes, I'm sure, stop fussing," insisted Boaz.

"Then why are you behaving so strangely around this woman?"

"Why?"

"Why?"

"Isn't it obvious? Look at her, the way she walks, talks laughs and smiles. She's radiant, composed, and so incredibly beautiful, don't you think so?" replied the infatuated Boaz.

The hired helps just looked at him as though Boaz had suddenly lost his mind which, of course, he had. But then, love makes men, even those of authority like Boaz, do the strangest things. Solomon wrote; *"There are three things that are too amazing for me, four that I do not understand; the way of an eagle in the sky, the way of a serpent on a rock, the way of a ship in the middle of the sea, and the way of a man with a maid."* (Proverbs 3: 18-19)

"One is very crazy when in love," said Sigmund Freud also.

Here was Boaz when faced by the beautiful Ruth. From the moment he'd caught sight of Ruth's charming smile, his behaviour became irrational. Certainly, any feeling of doubt regarding the future vanished. He knew Ruth was the one for him and he also knew he would remain in love forever. It was a case of "love at first sight", yet even more special because

God Himself was the author of it and Boaz began to believe this. Even before Tristan and Isolde, before Romeo and Juliet, and, yes, even before Mr Darcy and Elizabeth, Boaz and Ruth produced true love biblical style. Two people separated by historical bigotry and hostility, yet two people who defied every obstacle, and were destined to be together. The Bible is full of romantic legends providing stories in both the Old and New Testaments which were "love, at first sight" encounters, tales rivalling any modern-day Hollywood versions.

The Song of Songs, for example, is unique in its portrayal of passionate love between two lovers rejoicing in their intimacy. It includes affectionate lines like *"cover me with kisses, for your love is better than wine"* and *"your cheeks are so beautiful with those ornaments hanging beside them. Your neck is so lovely under that beautiful string of jewels"*.

Are such sentences appropriate to God's word?

Why not?

It is no sin to be tender, loving and kind.

Love is pure, and love is from God.

But the point of the song is not to highlight the importance of romantic encounters, but to provide additional emphasis, that of an allegory of the close union between Christ and His Bride, the Christian Church. The lasting love between Boaz (a native of the land of Israel) and Ruth (a foreigner from the land of Moab) became an epic love story, but ultimately their relationship symbolised far more than the union between a man and a woman, it would be illustrative of an enduring picture of the love between Almighty God and His creation.

The evidence of love is the desire to give, and Boaz would have given Ruth the world at this moment.

God's love is similar. Regarding our covenant relationship with Him, we did not make the first move, God did!

The Bible reminds us, *"We love him because he first loved us."* (1 John 4:9)

He gave up everything even to the point where He offered His only Son upon the cross to redeem His children which caused John to write; *"Behold, what manner of love the Father has bestowed upon us, that we should be called the sons of God."* (1 John 3:1)

Boaz is a representation of Jesus who is our Kinsman-Redeemer because he redeemed us at a high price when He shed His blood for us on the cross. Here was the purpose of Boaz in the life of Ruth — to bring restoration for her and Naomi. In the same way, as our redeemer, Jesus brings only blessings of wisdom, deliverance, restoration, provision, and liberty.

Boaz, therefore, is a splendid picture of the love of Christ the Saviour; while Ruth is a portrait of His bride. In his kindness and gentleness, Boaz is symbolic of the love of God, but Ruth represents those in need of a saviour.

While Boaz was thought to be much older than Ruth, age is no barrier when true love is at work, and God's purpose is being revealed. Their distinct cultural differences and other obstacles were no match for their love for each other either. From the moment their eyes met Boaz and Ruth were drawn to one another. It was a picture of enduring and pure love, exceptional joy, peace, and redemption — "a match made in heaven" as they say, and the embodiment of love at first sight!

Marriage was still a long way off, at this stage, after all they'd only just met, but everywhere Boaz looked around, love was in the air.

As he began to show his care, concern, and respect for Ruth, she knew he was treating her most gently and speaking with her so softly. It was a special feeling for her also.

Such generosity of spirit and gentleness of heart left Ruth amazed and caused her to fall on her face and bow herself to the ground before asking Boaz.

"Why are you so considerate of me? You know that I'm from another country and people?"

"I judge people on who they are, not where they live, Ruth. You have come here to seek refuge from God, and I am determined to help you find it. It has also been shown to me all that you have done for your mother-in-law since the death of your husband and how you have left your father and mother and the land of your birth and come to live with a people you know not."

"Thank you, Sir, for those comforting words and being so friendly towards me, especially given that I am a foreigner."

His reassuring smile told Ruth everything she needed to know. Boaz was already in love with her and Ruth with him. How could she not be in love? How could she resist such a man who would give her the sun, moon, and stars if he could?

Handsome, wealthy and kind, his tenderness and touching manners were everything she was looking for. Boaz was the answer to her and Naomi's most ludicrous prayer!

Still, Boaz felt the need to impress Ruth a little more. He couldn't afford to let such an opportunity slip through his hands. Time wasn't on his side, and he wasn't about to lose the girl of his dreams, so he finally galvanised the courage to ask an even bigger question.

After several days of monitoring her progress in the fields and speaking kindly with her, of observing her beautiful countenance, Boaz finally summoned the courage to ask the question every man fears to ask, "Would you like to join me at my residence for dinner tonight, Ruth? I could make you…"

"Love to, Sir, absolutely love to," Ruth quickly countered. Did I say that?, thought Ruth, What am I doing?

"I'd need somewhere to freshen up beforehand though, would you mind?" added Ruth.

Boaz smiled, and rejoiced inside. "Would I mind, Ruth? Of course, not, but please, from here on, no more Sir. You can call me Boaz and take as much time as you need. I've got all the time in the world."

Twelve

Guess who's coming to Dinner?

"And Boaz said unto her, at mealtime come hither,
and eat of the bread and dip thy morsel in the vinegar.
And she sat beside the reapers, and he reached her parched
corn, and she did eat, and was sufficed, and left." (Ruth 2:14)

Ruth arrived at the home of Boaz excited by her unexpected blessing, but sinister forces were already at work trying to rob her and Naomi of their badly needed breakthrough.

Their lives were linked to a divine plan, yet dark forces were out to try and abort it.

Just when people are about to be delivered, helped, and restored from their own personal dilemma's, someone or something is generally found lurking in the background ready and willing to thwart it. When the blessing of God shows up; the work of the enemy is never far away. The reaper sacked by Boaz was such a man. The worm had turned and sought revenge by spreading slander about Ruth to Naomi's nearest kinsman. Entering an adjacent field to the one he'd been working in, the reaper couldn't wait to enact retribution by breaking the news to someone in authority hoping his poisonous tongue would ruin Boaz and Ruth's search for happiness forever.

"Sir, I have been paid off by Boaz".

"Why? What have you done to deserve this?"

"You want to know my crime? Boaz has fallen in love with a woman and... wait for this — she's a foreigner."

"Who is this foreigner?"

"They say she's from Moab and her name is Ruth. She's supposed to be related to some woman called Naomi."

"Oh, no, not her! Don't tell me she's returned after all this time? She used to think she owned this place. I couldn't stand her"

"It appears so, Sir, how can I be of help to you in this matter?

"You already have helped, more than you know my dear brother. Don't worry; I will sort this out myself, but thank you: I'm very impressed with you. You have remained loyal to your people."

Such blind loyalty extended only to a leader, a brand of theology, and even a warped cause, but not to God. It wasn't the work of a loving God but the deception and hatred of a bitter enemy who uses discontented people and self-righteous people to hinder the lives of God's chosen servants. The root of the reapers dissatisfaction, of course, wasn't solely down to his dismissal by Boaz; it was also due to his deep-rooted prejudice and his intense dislike of foreigners. He was not just upset that Boaz, a prominent Israelite, had fallen for a foreigner like Ruth; he couldn't stomach the thought of a newcomer and outsider like Ruth poised to receive a blessing and remarkably hold a position in the land of Israel.

Many have said that discrimination is alive and well and some have reported it in evangelical circles. Immigration continues to be one of the most politically polarising issues around the world. The topic of immigration policy has been a staple of recent presidential debates, while Brexit has divided many within the nations and Church.

But the wisdom of the Bible is both timeless and straightforward and God would prove through the story of Ruth that He is more prominent and broader than our borders and her story shows she was part of a bigger plan and was made welcome in the family of God.

Despite the scheming by jealous and prejudicial patriots, Boaz remained focused, equally determined to find a place for Ruth at his top table. He refused to be intimidated by bigots in his generation.

What about us?

Do we stand up for the vulnerable and the outsider or seek popularity and position by keeping them estranged from society and the love of God? When the church rejects the foreigner it is no longer doing the work of a gracious God, but the work of the enemy.

Ruth had to undergo all of the latter.

She arrived at the residence of Boaz apprehensive being met by one of his most loyal servants. Ayah was a woman who had also come to Israel as a foreigner many years previously, yet Ayah ruthlessly rejected Ruth, placing her in another room to sit and wait alone for her new admirer.

Taking Boaz aside, she then whispered to her master in the hall:

"Your guest has arrived, and I don't like what I see here, Boaz. You are fascinated with a member of my race, and she will end up getting above herself. I know these people, and you will regret every bit of this."

Shocked and surprised, Boaz responded, "If I need your opinion, Ayah, I will ask for it."

"I mean it, Boaz; I've seen her type before breezing in here trying to steal your heart and your stuff. It will end in pain."

"Ayah, I appreciate your concern, really I do, but you are the last person I would have expected to say such a thing."

Boaz took his loyal aid Ayah aside, placed his hand on her shoulder, and said, "Listen to me, Ayah; you know I've always loved and respected you, but don't forget you are originally from Moab. How then could it be alright for me to love you and for God to redeem you and not Ruth? You need to stop and consider that? So, come on, what's on the menu tonight?"

"I haven't prepared a menu for tonight," responded Ayah sarcastically.

"I hope you have, and I hope it's a big spread. After all, we want to make sure we impress our guest from your part of the world."

Ayah shrugged her shoulders and sulked towards the kitchen.

Suddenly Boaz was met by another of his servants; only this hired help was more willing to rejoice in his newfound happiness.

"If you don't mind me saying, Sir, I've never seen you look so excited."

"You're right, Farah, I'm so happy I think I could burst."

"What has happened to you, Boaz?"

"To be honest, I don't know. I've never known anything like it. It was love at first sight. One moment I was standing in the barley field and the next she caught my eye."

"Imagine? You go to those fields every day and see only wheat, and today you find the woman of your dreams. Life is full of surprises and how true it is that we never know what a day brings forth, Boaz?"

"Yes indeed, Farah, and trust me, she is surprising in every way."

"What age is she?"

"I haven't a clue, but much younger than me and who cares anyway?"

"Well, they say women age differently to men, and I'm sure she's mature enough."

"Oh, she's mature alright, and extremely courageous. Along with her mother-in-law, Naomi, Ruth has gone through some tough experiences and prevailed. Oh, speaking of Ruth, I even forgot to tell you her name. Where is she?"

"In the next room, I believe, waiting for you, Boaz."

Farah then beamed the brightest of smiles at Boaz who gave the go-ahead for everyone to eat.

Once the guests assembled, faithful Ayah was incensed!

The other guests gave Ruth strange stares, too, leaving the poor girl wondering if coming to dinner was a good idea. As Ayah strutted back into the kitchen, she announced to the rest of the workers, "Well, guess what! Boaz has only gone and invited some foreigner from Moab to dinner."

"What?"

Ayah quickly returned to the top table with the food, finding Boaz drooling over his new love, recalling to the entire group how he and Ruth had met just a few days ago.

With stars in his eyes, Boaz confessed, "I fell in love with her, and even though it seems improbable, I think she fell in love with me, too."

Ruth blushed, bowed her head slightly, but notably she didn't deny it.

"Eat up, Ruth, you deserve it. You've worked hard today," insisted Boaz.

One mistrustful servant had already asked around about Ruth but had found her to be flawless and of immense character, so any objections to her presence wouldn't hold up for long, yet that didn't mean people were happy about the situation.

Meanwhile, Ayah continued to express her disapproval among her colleagues in the kitchen.

"I tell you, he's smitten with her and I think he means every word he says."

Another responded: "He may mean what he says, but Boaz doesn't know what he's doing. Imagine if this ends up in marriage? An Israelite joined to a Moabitess. Has Boaz considered the implications of this arrangement? If he marries her, she will become part of the covenant and the royal line!"

Meanwhile back at the dinner table things were progressing famously. By now, Boaz had Ruth in stitches with all his barley field stories. She could have listened to them all night but in the end, didn't want to overstay her welcome.

"I think I'd better be getting back to work. It's late, and I still haven't gathered enough."

"Not so fast," said Boaz. "You've done splendidly today, Ruth. Here, please take this extra grain to Naomi and tell her it's a gift from me."

Ruth smiled. "Thank you, Sir, that's so kind of you and thank you for the delicious meal."

"Believe me, Ruth, the pleasure was all mine."

Boaz accompanied her to the gate. It was a beautiful evening, and the sky was so colourful. Boaz sighed, a mixture of sheer happiness and content, a peaceful feeling that had eluded him for so long.

Who would speak first? No one wanted to break the beautiful silence between them. They were both happy-go-lucky at that stage.

"A red sky at night is a shepherd's delight."

"Yes, and I wonder what tomorrow has in store, Boaz?"

"I wonder indeed, my dear Ruth. I've enjoyed your company so much this evening. I'm sorry you're leaving."

"Not as sorry as I am, Boaz, it was quite an unexpected privilege for me."

The servants watched from the house as the pair then laughed incessantly and talked about everything under the sun.

Reluctantly, Ayah finally admitted Boaz was an enchanted man. "He's always been a happy person, and though I hate to admit it, until now I don't recall ever seeing Boaz so full of joy."

Just then he waved goodbye to Ruth, then returned to the house and immediately asked one of his hired servants, "How much did Ruth glean in the fields today?"

"Very little, probably not even enough for two people."

"I want you to take a few bushels and give her some grain, enough to last them quite a few days."

"Sir, forgive me, but why do you give her more when she hasn't asked for anything?"

Boaz smiled. "Do you know nothing of the love between a man and a woman my friend?

Ayah appeared again, only this time she kept quiet, but it was too late to avoid Boaz's displeasure. He hadn't been at all impressed with her performance before, during and after the dinner party.

"We enjoyed the food, Ayah; you are and always have been a marvellous cook, but I thought you might have been more civil to our guest, especially in light of our conversation earlier. In fact, all of you could have been more welcoming. I didn't expect to find such prejudice and opposition in this house."

"I'm sorry, Sir," said Ayah, "it's good to observe you full of joy, but I still don't like to see what I am seeing."

"And what are you seeing, Ayah? You are seeing Boaz, a single, lonely man, finally finding someone and you are not happy for him? I've never seen you so heated.

Are you jealous, Ayah?

"Me, jealous! I'm not jealous of her; I'm concerned for you, Boaz. You have such a great reputation, and everything will be ruined by one bad decision."

"Thank you for your concern, Ayah, but I can take care of myself."

"Are you sure, Sir?"

There was a fine line, of course, between being a loyal servant and telling your superior what to do.

"Let me tell you something, for thirty years there is no one I have respected more than you, Ayah, but your behaviour today has been out of order. You say a foreigner like Ruth doesn't belong in this country or my house, but you are here, and foreigners are in this country. What you say doesn't make sense. Our cultures may clash, Ayah, but there is room in God's kingdom for everyone who accepts Jehovah as the one true God, and you should never forget this."

"Now we are getting somewhere, Boaz. Who says Ruth has accepted our God? Who says she is part of God's kingdom?"

"Ruth left her homeland of Moab and followed Naomi to Bethlehem. She's already stated that Naomi's God is her God and Naomi's people her people. She has forsaken everything in her past to follow Naomi and our God. Have you heard her pray? What more does she have to do to meet your rigid religious standards, Ayah? Naomi has accepted Ruth and more importantly God accepts her, and therefore so should we."

Boaz had illustrated something to Ayah which may need to be heard again today.

The tale of an unlikely, yet passionate relationship which began in a barley field, between a Moabite widow Ruth and a well to do man from Bethlehem Boaz, is proof that people from different cultures can exist in peace and harmony — an important lesson for our 21st century multicultural society. The biblical romance between Boaz and Ruth, committed followers of the one true God, demonstrates how true love can overcome any obstacle; age, race, religion, and background.

How this also challenges our effortless assumptions and stereotypes about immigrants today and reminds us that, in this world, God's love and grace are not dictated by borders or lines on a map or any other hurdle.

The book of Ruth reveals how belonging can come not simply from blood but also by behaviour. Kindness and good character draw mutual kindness from others which results in inclusion for the stranger and the foreigner.

Boaz had first learned this truth from his mother. He was taught never to reject the stranger regardless of their faith. His mother Rahab had, at one point, been in a similar position to Ruth, an alien to the covenant of God, but through God's mercy, she too had been graciously grafted into God's family tree.

As a result, Rahab had educated Boaz as a young boy that it was wrong for Israelites like Boaz to act superior to heathens and unbelievers. She trained him how skin colour and religious background shouldn't prevent others from coming to know the one true God. That was hateful, stupid and wrong. How could he have known then, of course, that such teaching would enable him to receive outsiders with compassion and kindness to the extent where he ended up falling in love with one.

Throughout his life, he became especially conscious of things his mother had taught him regarding relationships with foreigners. Firstly, he was told when a foreigner resides among you in your land, do not mistreat them. According to the scriptures; *"Love them as yourself, for you were foreigners in Egypt."* (Leviticus 19:33-34), the foreigner residing among you must be treated as your native-born.

Boaz was also encouraged to leave food for the poor and the foreigner. This was in line with the laws of Israel which stated; *"When you reap the harvest of your land, do not reap to the very edges of your field or gather the gleanings of your harvest. Do not go over your vineyard a second time or pick up the grapes that have fallen. Leave them for the poor and the foreigner."* (Leviticus 19:9-10)

Here is evidence of God's love for the foreigner residing among the Israelites; evidence of how He defends the cause of the fatherless and the widow and shows compassion to the immigrant residing among them, giving them food and clothing. We are all His wonderful creation.

"And you are to love those who are foreigners, for you yourselves were foreigners in Egypt." (Deuteronomy 10:18-19)

Boaz was equally encouraged by his mother not to deprive foreigners of justice or treat them as outcasts; *"So I will come to put you on trial. I will be quick to testify against sorcerers, adulterers and perjurers, against those who defraud labourers of their wages, who oppress the widows and the fatherless, and deprive the foreigners among you of justice, but do not fear me,"* says the Lord Almighty. (Malachi 3:5)

And Boaz was additionally instructed to do whatever the foreigner requested; *"Do whatever the foreigner asks of you, so that all the peoples of the earth may know your name and fear you, as do your people Israel, and may know that this house I have built bears your Name."* (1 Kings 8:41-44)

And so, Boaz refused to attack other cultures! He knew this was a counterproductive act which would surely drive people away from the living God and perhaps at a time when they are in greatest need and even close to Salvation. It was this approach which helped cement a God-given relationship with someone from another nation — the girl from Moab, Ruth and bring about a most unexpected union between a man from Israel and a woman from Moab.

So far, Ruth hadn't opened up to Naomi about Boaz, but she couldn't keep it a secret any longer. And, so, returning from her third day of work at the barley fields, much later than the previous days, Ruth walked over the stones leading up to their humble abode beaming the brightest of smiles. Meanwhile, Naomi sprinted towards her daughter-in-law and embraced her with one gigantic hug.

"What has happened, my dear? Come inside and tell me. I'm so glad you're home safe. You've been away for ages today, how was it?"

"How was it? You've no idea, Mother. We are so blessed; I don't know where to start."

"What do you mean?"

Ruth handed Naomi the large bag of grain and smiled.

"Who was kind enough to let you glean in his field?"

"His name is Boaz. I think he likes me. He's been so kind to me."

They both laughed uncontrollably, and Naomi could sense that love was in the air.

Then suddenly it dawned on Naomi just who this Boaz was.

"I do believe Boaz is a relative of my husband, Elimelech. Yes, I am sure of it. I recall him now. He was always extremely kind as a little boy."

"He's still kind. Look what he has given us and he invited me to dinner earlier also."

"Dinner, are you serious? Did you accept?"

"Of course, Mother, you didn't expect me to look a gift horse in the mouth?"

"Ruth, you have found favour beyond my grandest expectations. Let's sort the grain and celebrate the goodness of God towards us. Let me hear all about your day and, of course, about this Boaz."

The pair hurried excitedly inside. The spread of grain on the table must have looked like a banquet compared to their usual paltry portions.

When you've been used to little and general lack and suddenly experience increase it's a welcome relief. But Ruth was feeling wonderful for all sorts of other reasons.

"Oh mother, he's so kind, calm and gentle and makes me feel like a princess."

"You are a princess, Ruth."

"When I lost Mahlon, I never thought I would feel this way again, Mother, but today it's as if I have come alive again."

"Tell me how you met?"

"I think It was love at first sight, Mother, at least for him. It probably took me a little longer."

"Less than a day?" Naomi joked.

"Less than an hour" Ruth replied excitedly. "Can I ask you a personal question, Mother? How long did it take for you to fall in love with Elimelech?"

"Not twenty minutes and I never loved another."

"Do you think it's possible, even right for me to love Boaz and forget Mahlon."

"You will never forget Mahlon, Ruth, but I don't believe God intends for you to be alone either. You are still young and must try to make a life for yourself again, Ruth, especially with Boaz."

"And you wouldn't be angry with me?"

"Not for a moment, my dear; on the contrary, I am overjoyed for you."

"Besides, this Boaz is a very wealthy man, Ruth."

"And good-looking, too, Naomi!"

"Yes, that always helps, Ruth!"

"Well, there is still one complication. I am a foreigner. Think about it, Naomi! What man in Bethlehem, including Boaz, would want me?"

"Ruth, any man with any sense, would jump at the chance of marrying you."

"Well, the reality is, I would have to leave you behind, and it's too soon for this."

Naomi pondered, then remarked, "Be careful, Ruth, you don't want to one day say it's too late either,"

"Then who knows! Maybe God can find a way to bless us together."

"You know what, Ruth, when God is in something, all things are indeed possible."

"They certainly are, Mother. After all, when I set out to work in those fields just a few days ago, who would have predicted such a wonderful outcome and in such a short space of time? You didn't even want me to go, remember?"

"That's true Ruth, that's so true! How merciful is our God? But then you showed such faith and courage going out to those fields and God has honoured you. You are right, today has proved to be extraordinary Ruth, a day that began with two strangers, two people from different economic and cultural upbringings, conversing and falling head over heels in love."

"Oh, I nearly forgot, Mother, did I tell you, there was opposition at the fields and in the house of Boaz, but you know what, I don't care anymore, it no longer matters to me what others think, surely it only matters what Boaz and I feel for each other."

"I agree, Ruth, if you are to be together as a couple, people here will probably be shocked and outraged, but if your love is real, you will both see off the doubters. You will learn to ignore them, even feel sorry for them, but a piece of advice Ruth — never, ever, give in to them."

Ruth breathed a sigh of relief, and went to say something else, but Naomi hadn't finished.

"Listen to me Ruth, if you are truly to be together, through every bit of prejudice, you will both need to cling to each other for your marriage to survive, but if you are both strong, you will make it and prove the doubters wrong."

"Marriage, are you serious, Mother? You think we could actually get married?"

"Of course, why not? If love is your magical ingredient, which it clearly appears to be, then surely my dear the only thing worse than getting married would be for two people, so deeply in love, not to get married at all."

Thirteen

Sit Still

"Sit still my daughter and see how the matter will fall."
(Ruth 3:18)

Aware that Ruth was ready to settle down again, Naomi sensed she was holding something back. Her astute mother in law knew well what it was.

"You're thinking of Mahlon, aren't you, Ruth."

"Yes, I've have had him on my heart a lot recently, but it's normal, right? We loved each other, and I still think of him so much."

"I understand, Ruth, but you need to think of yourself now. God has a purpose and plan for your life. He wouldn't have brought you all the way to Bethlehem with me for nothing. I believe He has someone else for you, Ruth and that someone is Boaz."

"What are you up to, Mother, and don't say nothing, I know that look. There's something else, isn't there?"

"You're right; there is something we need to discuss. I want you to have this."

Naomi handed Ruth a beautiful dress she'd kept for years for a special occasion; an occasion that had come, but sadly not for her. She knew the future belonged to her daughter now rather than herself.

Naomi was too old to dream of romance, but not for Ruth.

"What can I say, Mother? This dress is so stunning, and there was me thinking I had nothing to wear to the Barley Festival tonight."

"God always provides Ruth. I want you to go and dazzle that man Boaz, and trust me, in that dress; there will be only one girl in the room for him."

"Oh,Mother, you are simply the best. I don't deserve you."

"Yes, you do, Ruth. No one has ever been as faithful to me as you have been. The truth is Ruth you're the best daughter any mother could have. You've been better to me than seven sons. I couldn't love you anymore if you were my own. But listen carefully, Ruth, there's something else, and I need you to trust me on this."

"What is it, mother?"

"Go and get cleaned up and slip on your new outfit. Then, when you go to the festival, make sure you avoid Boaz at first."

"You mean tease him, Mother. I like the sound of that."

"Not quite, Ruth. I want you to watch him eat and drink until his heart is content. Stay out of his way and don't approach him no matter how tempted you feel. Then follow him out of the festival and when he lies down to sleep uncover his feet and lie down beside him."

"Are you serious, Mother? Think about what you're asking me to do. He will think badly of me. I'm not that sort of girl."

"Ruth, it's the custom of our people, and Boaz will give you a sign whether he's in favour or not. Trust me it's an appropriate thing to do."

"What if he's not a decent man and tries to take advantage of the situation?"

"Boaz follows the law of God. Believe me, Ruth; he will not break that, not even for you."

Ruth remained unconvinced. "This plan seems so illogical, even dangerous, and I just can't see how it can work, Mother."

"True, Ruth, but the ways of God are not our ways, and neither are His thoughts our thoughts. Sometimes we must do things which may even appear illogical to our God. You will be safe because God is in this, we have to trust Him."

"All right, all right," said Ruth. "As crazy as it sounds, I will do as you say. You've always been right before so why not again."

"God is always right, Ruth. His ways are perfect."

After anointing herself, Ruth looked radiant in her stunning blue dress and matching footwear. Her hair was pinned up highlighting her face. Amidst the music, dancing and laughter, Ruth suddenly realised why Naomi had told her not to approach Boaz. It was tempting to make a move for Boaz, she wanted to talk with him so much, but her mother-in-law knew better and had instructed Ruth to hold back and wait until later. If anyone had learned to wait patiently for the Lord, it was Naomi. She, more than most, had learned the hard way. Those desperate times when she didn't know how they were going to survive had shown Naomi how God is faithful when we reach a place of immense trust and peace.

So Ruth stuck to the plan. As Boaz left the festival, she slipped out behind him and followed him until he'd fallen asleep. Concealed behind thick grass and trees, Ruth couldn't take a chance on being seen. Tongues would wag like wildfire damaging her well-respected character. Such a prospect was unthinkable making her actions precarious and even foolish.

"Oh, Lord, Naomi is full of wisdom, but surely this idea is a step too far," she prayed.

As she progressed to where Boaz slept, her heart skipped a beat with worry. Then, quietly, she uncovered his feet and lay down for the night beside him. It was a dark corner of a field, but the stars were out, and it was warm and cosy. Boaz never moved the entire night. Ruth lay and stared at him only realising then just how handsome he was, and how much she longed to be with him, eventually falling asleep too.

As morning broke, Boaz, startled by the sight of Ruth at his feet, jumped quickly up and asked:

"Who are you?"

"It's me, Boaz. Ruth?"

"Why are you here, Ruth?"

"Because you are our kinsman redeemer and I recall your kind and tender words 'may the Lord protect me under the spread of his wings.' Those words so touched my heart. Is it wrong for me to ask the same of you?"

Boaz couldn't believe what he was hearing. The love of his life, the girl of his dreams, the woman he'd hoped and prayed would one day become his wife was suddenly lying at his feet.

They stared at each other for what seemed like an eternity until Boaz smiled, "Was this Naomi's idea?"

Ruth's reluctance to reply was a giveaway, and they both fell apart laughing.

"I tell you, that woman is incorrigible," said Boaz.

"Why have you chosen to lie beside me, Ruth? Your beauty and true character mean you could have anyone, yet you chose me. Why?"

"Why Boaz? Are you serious? No one has ever shown me so much love and kindness as you have. You have shown us so much mercy, and I am yours forever from this point forward."

Kindness brings its own reward while compassion is a powerful magnet for others.

Kindness more than anything had won Ruth's heart. Yes, Boaz was handsome, yes, he was wealthy, and yes, he had position and popularity, but goodness was his best attribute.

Never underestimate the power of kindness! It can soften the hardest of hearts. It can unite opposing people and nations like nothing else. Meanwhile, Boaz just stared at Ruth in the same way he'd done the first day they'd met, before sharing for the first time his heart with his one true love.

"Oh Ruth, I've waited so long to tell you this. I've loved you from the day our eyes met. You must have noticed. In fact, I've thought of nothing else but you since. I even prayed that God would give you to me because I couldn't imagine a life without you, Ruth."

"Then God has surely answered your prayer, Boaz because neither could I imagine life without you."

Boaz's expression changed, as he dropped his head in disappointment. It wasn't the reaction Ruth had expected, especially at such a romantic moment.

Something was wrong.

"Is everything alright, Boaz? I thought you would be pleased."

"I am pleased, I'm ecstatic, but everything is not alright, Ruth. You see, I've some bad news for you. I'm not your closest kinsman. There's a closer relative, and he's not happy with how I've reached out to you."

"Who is this man you speak of Boaz?"

"It's the brother of Elimelech, but I don't want you to worry because I think there's a way to sort this out, although it will take much faith. I want to be with you Ruth, believe me, I do, but I can't touch you until the law says I can. So I'm asking you to return to your mother and wait."

"Naomi told me to wait, and now you are asking me to wait, why does life always entail having to wait?"

"I agree, Ruth, waiting is not for the faint-hearted, especially when you desire someone as much as I do you."

Ruth needed to leave before the sun came up. After all, they'd just spent the night together, and even though nothing intimate or illicit had taken place, Boaz knew that people are people and gossip would have been inevitable. But not before Boaz gave her yet another gift of barley and provision for her and Naomi. This time Boaz lavished her with six measures of grain — the equivalent of sixty days supply of food.

"Oh, Boaz, what can I say? Your love and care for us are overwhelming."

"I cannot disagree, Ruth. You do know I love you?"

"And I love you too, Boaz," said a tearful Ruth as she parted from the new love of her life to begin her unpleasant period of waiting.

As Ruth returned to open the front door of their small home, not surprisingly Naomi was anxious for her daughter in law; her eyes filled with expectancy and hope.

"Well, don't just stand there, how did things go?" she asked.

Ruth looked a little sad at first, mischievously misleading her mother-in-law who had prayed continually for this union between Ruth and Boaz.

Suddenly Ruth beamed the brightest smile and shouted "Oh Mother, everything went perfectly. You were right, Boaz is a decent man, he was with me all night and didn't touch me, and we are so in love, but...."

"But what, Ruth?

"There's a major complication; he's not our closest kinsman."

"I already know, Ruth. It's Elimelech's brother, and he's not a nice man."

"You knew?"

"Yes, unfortunately, and I thought this might be a problem for us."

"Boaz told me he is a difficult individual, but he said he would fight for us, mother."

"I believe him, he is an honourable man indeed Ruth, and now that he loves you he will fight all the more, but we have a part to play too, Ruth, we must pray and be still."

"Be still? It is a golden opportunity for us; we need to act, mother, not be still."

"No, Ruth, sometimes remaining still and leaving things with God is far more powerful than anything you or I might do."

Then, to Naomi's surprise and delight, for the first time since returning to Bethlehem, Ruth took Naomi's hand and began to call upon the name of the Lord. It was a prayer that not only touched the heart of Naomi but also confirmed just how far Ruth had travelled from the days of following the gods of Moab to now serving the one true God Jehovah.

As Ruth closed her eyes and lifted her head towards heaven, she prayed. "We come to the most high God — the only true and living God — and we say thank you, Father, for your amazing love and mercy towards us. Thank you for your great provision and for sending Boaz into our lives. Thank you for the day and hour you sent Naomi into my life for without her I may never have got introduced to you gracious heavenly Father. Who is like, unto you, Oh God and we trust you completely for everything including this situation with Elimelech's brother. Is anything too hard for the Lord? As we give this situation into your capable hands, please undertake on our behalf, and we will return with thanksgiving and praise in our hearts. Amen."

Ruth's prayer made it so much easier for Naomi to give her the next instruction, a most potent and profound sentence — one which is not easy to adhere to in most instances — but something all of us are required to do at crucial times in our lives.

"Sit still my daughter and see how the matter will fall." (Ruth 3:18)

In other words, from here on, do nothing! Leave everything to God and let God decide the future! Here is the hardest thing a believer can do — nothing!

Ruth would have found this hard, but Naomi had long learned to leave things in God's hands.

Moab had taught her this.

She was determined not to make the same mistake as she and Elimelech had made when leaving Israel.

Those who don't learn from past mistakes are destined to make them again, and Naomi wasn't about to make any further impulsive moves.

She preferred to wait on God's timing rather than trust in her own judgment.

What's interesting is the fact that she didn't recommend Ruth telling Boaz a sad story, even though both she and Ruth had a tragic story to tell. They could also, with some justification, have cried poverty, but didn't. Neither did Naomi encourage Ruth to get a ring on her finger ASAP. The words "go for it, Ruth, he's handsome and wealthy, what more could you want" weren't rhetoric used by Naomi. Instead, she simply asked Ruth to 'sit still' and see what materialised. Waiting on God is the hardest thing a child of God can do, but it is also the most rewarding. The book of Hebrews says; *"He is a rewarder of those who diligently seek him."* (Hebrews 11:6)

Of course, there are times when we need to make decisions, big decisions, when waiting is not appropriate, yet frequently we are too quick to make important choices leaving no room for the guidance of God. Psalm 40:1 states; *"I waited "patiently" for the Lord and he inclined unto me and he heard my cry."*

It proved Naomi's firm conviction, too. Naomi didn't just learn to wait; she had mastered the art of "waiting patiently?"

Or, waiting until waiting seems impossible anymore. She believed with all her heart that God answers prayer, and if she waited on Him, He would show up with the right answer at the right time. She had wanted with all her heart to wait in Israel with Elimelech but was forced to run ahead of God and the consequences were disastrous.

As an ambitious but naive teenager, Joseph desired to see his dreams fulfilled, yet had to wait for over twenty years to experience such a reality. Joseph was made to wait for an extra two full years before being released from prison where he had already spent around eleven years.

Lying in that dark, cold dungeon, for something he hadn't done, one day a genuine opportunity arose to get his case heard. A baker and a butler both needed their dreams interpreted, and Joseph possessed such a gift. He could have refused by his injustice, but there appeared to be no anger dwelling within his heart. Instead, he interpreted the dreams for both men before asking the butler not to forget him when he was before the king.

As so often happens with those we've been good too, the butler did indeed forget Joseph condemning him to a further period of misery and frustration in jail.

What more could Joseph have done?

He had put his suffering to one side to help others, and he had used the gift God had given him to its fullest capacity, yet still, he remained behind bars. Perhaps it was during the following two years where Joseph learned the beauty and benefit of sitting still and leaving his situation and issues at the feet of God for nowhere after this period do we read that Joseph contacted the correctional officers, the King or anyone else. It appears he did not protest his innocence any further and handed his life over to the Lord. What was the result of his sitting still? The Bible states how when *"two full years had passed,"* and in the same way the baker and the butler became troubled by dreams, the King, Pharaoh, also was unable to interpret his dreams. He'd called every magician and soothsayer in the land, and no one had an answer to his riddles. It was here that the butler finally remembered Joseph and told the king about his prolific gift to interpret dreams causing the king to send for him. The Bible records; *"Then Pharaoh sent and called Joseph, and they brought him out hastily out of the dungeon; and he shaved himself, and changed his raiment, and came in unto Pharaoh."* (Genesis 41:14)

Note how Pharaoh sent and called for Joseph, it wasn't the other way around. Are you currently trying to organise, orchestrate or scheme your deliverance from a particular situation?

Why not hand it over to God?

For almost thirteen years Joseph may well have tried to manage his deliverance, manipulating various people to gain an audience with the king and all to no avail, but when he handed his plight over to God and sat still, when he realised only God and Him alone could help free him, the answer soon arrived. All along the Lord had planned for Joseph not only to be released from the dungeon but to enjoy the highest position in the land of Egypt of Prime Minister. It was all part of God's great purpose and master plan for his child, his family and a nation. It sounds silly but you know what — God knows what He's doing? He requires us to sit down, be still and know that He is God and is in control.

When was the last time you sat still and diligently sought the Lord? Not just when you're in trouble, but in general? To seek God diligently and trust him completely takes "careful and persistent work or effort".

It takes work and effort and faith to seek God and to wait for his timing, to leave things in His hands. It takes enormous trust and hope, but due to her painful past, Naomi now possessed such qualities. This woman must have looked back in horror at the times she and Elimelech had moved ahead of God, rather than wait for His intervention.

Ours is a generation like Elimelech's, obsessed with self and no longer willing to wait. We live in what is known as "the microwave society." Our meals must be ready in less than one minute, or we go to McDonald's for a quick fix. No one wants to queue up anymore; our shopping arrives at the front door via some internet service following the click of a button and people can't wait to get married, to have babies, can't wait to go on holiday, and can't wait for anything. No one wants to wait, but not waiting can cost so much.

Anyone trying to meet a deadline when the computer decides to go slow will know the feeling exactly. We sit staring at the computer screen watching the little mouse burling round and round leaving us with only two choices. Try and force the issue by thumping the computer which always ends up costing more time or hit the wait button until the problem is sorted out.

Life's choices are similar. Many choose to ignore the wait button. They still believe too much in their strength and abilities, and so, like poor old Elimelech, they press on with their own agendas, only to rue the same horrible consequences that Naomi's husband and family experienced later on.

We may not have suffered death, in the way Elimelech and his sons did, but the same end and devastation have visited many ministries and personal situations due to the inability to sit still and wait on God. The advice given by Naomi to her daughter in law Ruth was, therefore, precious and godly counsel — *wait, sit still, pray and trust God.*

Breakthrough and intimacy with God require patience and trust. We must learn to wait and quiet the clatter and enter his stillness for, in such silence, we find the answer to our everyday dilemmas.

Elijah did not get his response in the earthquake, wind or fire but in the "still small whisper".

Similarly, perhaps God is asking you to wait on Him to give you your answer?

Ruth didn't just wait, though; she also vowed to do all that Naomi asked of her. She was not just trusting and patient. Notably, she was obedient. If God is asking us to sit still and wait and see how the matter will fall, are we prepared to obey his command and do this?

Solomon wrote; *"Trust in the Lord with all thy heart and lean not unto your understanding. In all thy ways acknowledge Him, and He shall direct thy paths."*

Waiting was a commandment regularly given to God's people in both the Old and New Testaments. In the Old Testament, the most quoted verse on waiting is in the book of Isaiah. Most of us can recite this verse verbatim, what we often find more difficult is living it out in our lives. *"They that wait upon the Lord shall renew their strength, they shall mount up with wings like eagles, they shall run and not be weary, and they shall walk and not faint."* (Isaiah 40:31)

The New Testament book of Luke outlines how Jesus told the disciples to *"Tarry (wait) ye in the city of Jerusalem until ye be endued with power from on high."*

Jesus is explicitly saying that unless his followers wait on God, they lack power for ministry. They will have no real anointing, no clout and no influence, no breakthrough!

People ask why the church is so ineffective today; why we no longer see growth and miracles and transformation like former days. Generational change is often the reason given, but the answer might well be because leaders are no longer prepared to wait on God. On the other hand, all Bible greats like Naomi and Ruth were people who knew how to wait.

Moses was told to *"Stand still and see the Salvation of the Lord"*, and he obeyed, and God opened the sea. The laws of nature decreed that such a feat was impossible, but by faith, obedience and patience, Moses and God proved otherwise.

Mary remained at the tomb of Jesus when everyone else had gone home, but her faith was rewarded when she saw the Risen Lord.

Psalm 46:10 says; *"Be still and know that I am God."* One of the Hebrew renderings of this verse is, "Take your hands off it" or "Let go and let God."

Mary waited at the feet of Jesus and received the best part, but Martha stayed burdened by the cares of life and tried to exist on her strength alone. The result was what we call today "spiritual burn-out."

Despite being in a most precarious situation, think of how tempting it would have been for Naomi and Ruth to rush things with Boaz, yet Naomi suggested they should instead trust God to see how the matter would fall. What a great woman of faith she proved? There was a storm raging in their lives, but they calmed the storm by faith and trust in the living God and their kinsman redeemer soon arrived.

Fourteen

Grace is Greater

"But where sin abounded,
grace abounded much more."
(Romans 5:20)

Boaz had lost his appetite. He couldn't contemplate eating until he'd worked out a way to be with his one true love, Ruth. It was all he could think of.

With both Naomi and Ruth now resting, Boaz, the owner of the barley field, went to work immediately, initiating actions, executing them and speaking on Ruth's behalf.

To show favouritism to a foreigner was a risk, but Boaz was in love, a love so great for Ruth he would have given up anything.

He didn't usually leave his fields during the day, but the matter was too important to ignore. His entire future happiness depended upon it.

Ever faced a task more pressing than your daily agenda? Ever had an urge to get something done before it slipped through your hands no matter what else is demanded of you?

Here was Boaz.

"I'm going to attend to business, folks, I'll be back later," he declared to his servants.

His loyal staff knew something was up but didn't dare ask what. Boaz was a conscientious man who never ignored his work but neither had Boaz any intentions of explaining himself. He'd already encountered enough opposition to his apparently "unsuitable" relationship with Ruth and the matter was not up for discussion.

Ayah, who, of course, had objected to Boaz and Ruth's association over dinner, came sprinting out of the house, but this time her words were much more comforting and contrite.

"Boaz, please forgive me for the other night, I'm sorry for the way I behaved, it was wrong and intolerant of me. It's clear you are in love and intend to fight for Ruth so I promise to pray for God's will to be accomplished in your life."

Boaz stopped, looked back and smiled, then spoke, "Thank you, Ayah, you've no idea how that has helped me. I couldn't bear it if you weren't happy for me."

"I only wanted the best for you." she replied with a tear in her eye.

"I know, Ayah, everything is okay, really it is. Go back to your work. I'm blessed to have such a loyal and faithful servant as you," insisted Boaz.

Heading towards the city gate where the elders were waiting, his heart was pounding. Not through fear of what might happen to him; instead, Boaz was uptight in case things didn't go as planned regarding his desire to have Ruth as his wife. If things went the wrong way, it would be back to porridge for Boaz; back to the single, lonely life he'd become familiar.

A large crowd had gathered as Boaz approached the gate. He spotted Naomi and Ruth and suddenly Naomi gestured to him with her hands clasped, reminding Boaz that she was praying for him. After all, this was a huge moment for all three of them. Boaz needed a wife, Ruth needed a husband, and Naomi required selling the land that belonged to her late husband, Elimelech. Ariel, a friend of Elimelech's brother, Yosef, had joined the crowd and noticed how Boaz had acknowledged both Naomi and Ruth.

"Do you know, Naomi, Ariel?"

"Yes, I remember her, Boaz."

"That's interesting; because I've noticed you haven't exactly been very welcoming to her since she returned."

"That's enough, Boaz, he maybe didn't have the opportunity," Naomi interrupted.

Naomi understood that some people were entitled to be slightly off with her and that not everyone felt able to welcome her back so quickly.

Nevertheless, Boaz rolled his eyes, refusing to buy Naomi's gracious excuse on behalf of Ariel. There was no more time to talk anyway. The elders had already assembled, and things quickly deteriorated for Boaz. Facing a firing squad in the public square, Boaz — a pillar of society and local statesman — was called a traitor and accused of giving away half of his grain to a woman from Moab.

The chief elder summoned Boaz to the top of the steps.

"We've heard reports about you Boaz which has concerned us. It has come to our attention that you've shared and given away your grain to a foreigner, a severe breach of our laws and an unthinkable act of treason. Is this true?"

"According to our laws, it is not wrong to help strangers, and so I haven't done anything wrong," Boaz calmly replied.

"Do not play this down, my friend; it is a serious matter; besides we have enough information to bury you," added another angry elder.

"Like what?" retorted Boaz.

"You'll see."

Rather than seeking to cover up for Boaz and protect him as one of their brethren, these men seemed more concerned with exposing him to the entire town, and even to the point of excommunication. Although Boaz hadn't sinned and retained an unblemished character; in their prejudice and dislike for foreigners, this group of self-righteous elders were still prepared to report that he had done wrong and thus make him face public ridicule and the resulting consequences.

"Listen up, people of Israel, this man Boaz is nothing short of a traitor. His intentions are not honourable. He plans to give half of all his grain to a foreigner," announced the irate brother of Elimelech, Josef.

The crowd gasped and gossiped for what seemed like an eternity before further accusations and suggestions emerged.

"It has also come to some ears how this man even slept with the foreigner. Stone him to death, that is the penalty for treason and giving away stuff to foreigners," shouted another angry elder.

Boaz protested. "That's a scandalous accusation and there's no truth in any of it, nor in that harsh law you quote. While I am guilty of welcoming and supporting the foreigner, my only motive is to help Ruth by purchasing the field of Elimelech and thus becoming Ruth's Kinsman Redeemer. Are you religious zealots aware that God loves and welcomes foreigners?"

It was a brave speech which lost Boaz many friends and admirers. He'd only spoken the truth but was already suffering the consequences. Nevertheless, his strong stand helped save the house of Elimelech from poverty and ruin, but Josef remained incensed, determined to thwart Boaz's plan. He'd convinced himself that he alone had the right to his brother's fortune and even choice of wife. Just as Naomi had suspected all along, Elimelech's brother became an obstacle opposing the idea on the grounds that he was entitled to the inheritance because he was the true kinsman. When he realised, however, he would have to redeem the wife of his brother's house, the Moabitess named Ruth, he fell right into Boaz's trap.

"You can't do this," insisted Josef. "It is my right and only mine. Being the closest relative, Elimelech's land and his wife belong to me."

"Not so," said the chief elder, a statement which not only stunned Josef, but the watching crowd.

"You have not interpreted the law properly, Josef. It is not the widow of Elimelech you redeem, but the widow of Mahlon, Ruth, or you will forfeit your right to anything."

Josef was never going to redeem Ruth so, as was the custom of the laws of Israel, if someone didn't want to redeem another, they had to remove their sandal and give it to the next kinsman who, in this case, was Boaz. Realising Ruth was a "bridge too far", Josef removed his sandal and angrily threw it at a smirking Boaz.

Then to make things even more legal, Boaz, a kinsman by blood, instantly announced that he would marry Ruth, thus securing both her and Naomi's future and the house of Elimelech forever.

Cheers went up from the assembled crowd, many of whom appeared delighted for Boaz and Ruth, but equally mortified by the behaviour of Elimelech's brother, especially his unseemly display of throwing his sandal across the floor in disgust.

Throughout the entire hearing the behaviour and intention of Boaz was most honourable. The actions of Boaz helped therefore to preserve the name both in the folklore of the population (as told in the book of Ruth) and in the line of David.

By redeeming the land and Ruth, we see here a picture of the first of three redeemers in the story of Naomi, which is Boaz.

He presents an almost perfect picture of Jesus, our heavenly kinsman-redeemer. For when we rest in the Lord, just like Ruth and Naomi did with Boaz, He will fight for us, and He will come through for us. All we need to do in return is trust him for our provision and enjoy His love for us. Incredibly, through it all, Ruth had just sat still and rested. She did nothing, and yet ended up with everything!

She trusted in God's way, not her way and received exceedingly more than she could ever have expected.

The story of how Ruth becomes part of the people of Bethlehem is more than a tale of romance, and redemption, it is more than an epic tale of courage and self-determination, because it involves a community review of the laws and traditions that shape it and it introduces the reader to the unstoppable grace of God. There is much for our generation to learn from the actions of Ruth and indeed Boaz in this part of the story.

Grace is always higher and greater than harsh law!

Due to events involving this one woman named Ruth, the people ultimately agree to reshape their laws to expand the scope of those who are included within their protection. And so, by the end of the story, a foreign woman is contained within the embrace of the community and becomes an ancestor to their greatest king.

Like Rahab, who risked her life assisting the Israelites, similarly Ruth, because of her excellent character and blessed life, becomes a woman of legendary Bible status.

But another, vital and timely principle is also established here, namely that the law should ensure compassion, and if it doesn't, it must be changed.

Here again there is genuine relevance to our generation. Some of our churches today are bringing the truth without love, while it seems others prefer to teach love without truth. The perfect law is one which has the balance of both grace and truth. Boaz was a man, like Jesus, full of grace and truth.

One of my favourite movies is the film entitled 'The Terminal'. When Victor Navorski, (Tom Hanks) an eastern European tourist, arrives in JFK airport in New York, war breaks out in his country, and he finds himself caught up in international politics. Because of the war, Department of Homeland security won't let him enter or exit the United States; and so he finds himself trapped at JFK — indefinitely.

While living at the airport for almost a year, Viktor falls in love with flight attendant, (Catherine Zeta-Jones), but the movie brings to light more than a love story and a hilarious plot. It also teaches top agent Frank Dixon (Stanley Tucci) a vital life lesson about the importance of understanding when to uphold and maintain the law and when to show compassion and mercy to his fellow man.

As he attempts to climb the corporate ladder, however, by sticking rigidly to the rule, and showing no sympathy or familial consideration, rather than impressing his superiors, Dixon is denied the promotion he so desperately craves. Homeland security laws were so tight, Dixon maintained throughout that he was only "doing his job", but he soon learned that if there cannot be genuine "exceptions to the rule," common sense gets ignored and people are made to suffer needlessly.

It appears Boaz took a tradition or law within Judah that was designed to provide protection, economically and socially for Judahite women who were widowed and he expands its application to include Ruth, a foreigner.

Technically the law applies neither to Naomi nor Ruth, but Boaz acts as if it does. Presumably, he does this because he knows the community is aware of the excellent character of Ruth (3:10-11).

The law of levirate marriage as initially understood did not embrace Ruth because she was a foreigner, yet Boaz acts to extend even this in the light of her vulnerability and her integrity. Law in the Hebrew Bible was intended to ensure kindness in the community, yet in this instance, just like the initial US immigration policy, the unintended outcome of a strict application was unkindness. It was motivation enough for Boaz to seek to change it

And, in a sense, he appears to argue that if the Law doesn't provide protection for people like Ruth, and include them within its scope, then it should, and if necessary, it should be expanded or adjusted to do so.

Here is a timeless principle about God — His grace is always higher than harsh law.

Grace provides a way when there is no way and grace offers another chance for someone to shine, even when they either don't deserve it or have no right to it. No one can keep the laws of God and no one deserves God's Salvation, but God still made a way for everyone to be saved through the death and sacrifice of His Son Jesus at the cross. No sin is too powerful for God's grace to reach.

Paul wrote; *"But where sin abounded, grace abounded much more."* (Romans 5:20)

When a politician fails to meet the moral standards expected of them, or when a preacher messes up, they are often described as having "fallen from grace." Because they have sinned so publicly, people assume they are deemed to have fallen from grace. But God wants you to understand that when you sin, you have not fallen from grace, but fallen into grace. His grace is available at precisely the time when you need it.

What am I saying!

God's grace is always greater than sin and harsh law, and He is ready and willing to restore even the worst mistakes in our lives.

The Bible is full of stories of how prostitutes, tax collectors, and general sinners mercifully received the grace of God inspiring them all to follow the Lord. Only the grace of God can defeat and destroy sin.

Paul also wrote; *"For sin shall not have dominion over you, you are not under the law, but under grace."* (Romans 6:14)

Once we realise that grace is greater than sin and misinterpreted law, once we accept that God's grace has made us righteous in Him, sin will truly die in our lives.

Sin does not and can never stop the grace of God. If God's grace could have been defeated by the devil or by sin, then Christ would not have come to the place called Calvary to redeem sinners from their sins. In his early days of school, a little boy was regularly in trouble with the teacher and brought before the headmaster more times than he could remember. In those days, the punishment for unruly behaviour was what we referred to as "six of the best". The teacher would use a strong cane to whack the children who had been causing trouble. One day after the boy had been caught fighting with a fellow pupil; he was summoned to the gymnasium where most of the canings were carried out away from the sight of the other children.

On this particular occasion he was surprised because the teacher said he wanted to teach the boy a lesson but not in the usual way. When he asked the teacher what the lesson was he replied "grace."

The boy was told to face the wall, put out his hands and close his eyes. At this point he became extremely frightened because he had no idea what grace was. It could have been an even harsher punishment than the one he'd been expecting. At that moment the boy heard the first blow and crack of the cane but felt no pain. Then there was another blow and still no pain or feeling in his hands. The blows continued to pour down until six had been completed. When the boy opened my eyes, he could scarcely believe it.

His teacher's hands were red and swollen because he had taken the punishment on himself from another teacher. Immediately the little boy began to weep. The teacher reached his swollen hands towards the face of the boy and said one word — "grace".

He told him never to forget that word because it could one day change his life, but through the action of the teacher, it already had. The boy's thinking changed from rebellious to repentance. The teacher had presented Jesus on a cross shedding His blood for his sins and for no other reason than grace.

The word grace is described in the dictionary as "elegance and smoothness of movement," but in theological terms the word grace is simply "unmerited favour." It is the help or strength given through the atonement of the Lord Jesus Christ. Grace is a gift from a heavenly father given through His Son, Jesus Christ. The very centre and core of the Bible is the doctrine of the grace of God. Grace is the love of God shown to the unlovely, the peace of God given to the restless and the undeserved favour of God.

John Stott said, "Grace is the love that cares, and stoops and rescues." Paul Zahl wrote "Grace is the unconditional love towards a person who doesn't deserve it." Unfortunately, ours is a world where earning deserving and merit all feature high on the list, but it only results in condemnation and judgement. Everyone therefore requires and needs grace.

Judgement destroys.

Only grace brings life.

Sadly, some people and even preachers in the church today are uncomfortable with the message of grace. It seems they prefer to earn, work and justify their place in heaven, but Salvation is a free gift which only requires trust and faith in the finished work of Jesus. To dilute God's grace is to come against the person who provides it — the Lord Jesus Christ. There's a new movement of grace preachers and people on the planet today who are determined to bring the truth of the gospel to the church while many who stubbornly continue to teach religion in place of the goodness and grace of God are becoming more and more redundant. What is happening? God is sitting one down and raising up another to make way for His glorious message of love and grace. In the same way that Boaz rescued Naomi and Ruth by becoming their Kinsman Redeemer, so, too, Jesus by His amazing grace and sacrifice at the cross came to redeem every one of us.

How high is the grace of God?

It cannot even be measured. Joseph Prince puts it this way, "The grace of God is bigger, deeper, wider and more powerful than the entire world's sin put together."

Such grace has touched the lives of millions and will continue to do so in this dispensation of grace. It certainly touched the lives of both Naomi and Ruth, especially when the Almighty sent Boaz their way. Here were two women, destitute and alone and with little hope left in the world until the grace of God arrived and transformed their situations.

God's grace proved greater than Elimelech's mistakes, it proved greater than racial prejudice and ageism, it proved greater than cultural barriers, it defeated any opposition to Boaz and Ruth's union, and it brought unity where unity hadn't existed before.

This presents us with an obvious consideration; namely, what are the implications of the actions of Boaz in his generation for us as a community facing into life in the 21st century and the complexities of our world? Valuable lessons can be learned at this time from this Old Testament story of Boaz, Ruth and Naomi. Do we show and extend the true grace of God to people of every background and situation? While nations need to secure their borders, while there's a requirement to protect one's people, the laws of any country should also allow for friendly welcome and hospitality to people in great need, as was the case when Elimelech and Naomi's family and other Israelites who'd arrived in Moab all those years previously.

By making way for Ruth, Boaz was merely returning the same kindness to her which Moab had extended to Naomi and her family after they had emigrated from Israel following the famine, something which allowed Ruth to receive divine blessing going from leftovers to owning the entire field and becoming part of the family of God. And, by marrying Ruth, who maintained the family name, Boaz enabled her to conceive a child — one whose delivery would prove to be no ordinary birth.

Fifteen

No Ordinary Birth

"Then Naomi took the child and laid him on her bosom, and became a nurse to him. Also, the neighbour women gave him a name, saying, 'There is a son born to Naomi.' And they called his name Obed; He is the father of Jesse, the father of David." (Ruth 4:16-17)

The marriage between Ruth and Boaz took place shortly afterwards and their undying loyalty to God and each other showered blessings on their family they could only have dreamed.

It wasn't long either before Ruth began to involve herself in the running of their home, quite an undertaking. Having become the wife of one of Bethlehem's wealthiest men, a man revered and respected at the gate, Ruth's lifestyle was about to change forever and, in more ways than one!

While Boaz was known for sitting among the elders of the land, Ruth kept their home in a manner which, at times, left even Boaz speechless. Like the Proverbs 31 woman, strength and dignity were her clothing and, when she opened her mouth, wisdom came forth, while the teaching of kindness was on her tongue.

"Oh, Ruth, many women have done excellently, but you surely surpass them all," Boaz would tell his new wife every night.

Ruth was as faithful to Boaz as she had been to Naomi; never idle or lazy, she worked tirelessly and feared and praised the Lord. She wasn't perfect, but here was a woman of moral fibre, faithfulness, and virtue. Boaz trusted her with his life, for no matter what, his wife continually seemed to bring forth fruit. While she'd adapted well as the wife of Boaz, another surprise from the Lord would introduce her to something else, something she'd dreamed about regularly after the loss of her former husband Mahlon — motherhood!

After Ruth fell sick, and Boaz became concerned. It was a complaint out of the blue, but Ruth and Naomi knew well what the problem was. Naomi had been in the town when word spread that Ruth had become poorly. Rushing back home she found Boaz in a state of turmoil, yet all of Naomi's experience as a mother and a woman informed her that things were probably not as perilous as Boaz had assumed. Nevertheless, she encountered a man in complete and utter misery.

"I can't understand what's the matter, Naomi. Ruth can't keep anything down, and she's so weak. Her temperature is through the roof, and I'm concerned about her and don't know what to do."

"Don't panic, Boaz, I know exactly what to do. Please leave us alone for a while."

"Why, what is going on, Naomi?"

"We are going to pray, Boaz. Now please, leave us together until this is sorted."

Naomi pointed to the door, urging Boaz to trust her and eventually he took the hint shuffling slowly, yet reluctantly outside.

As Naomi removed her headscarf and took the hands of Ruth, Boaz was pacing up and down the pathway, where he, too, began to pray. Never before had this strong man seemed so feeble or become so frightened, not even the time when he had to face that wretched religious firing squad in the town centre. That was a cakewalk compared to the distress Boaz was feeling inside. He'd won the hearts of the people that day and Ruth, so the thought of losing her wasn't an option; it would be unthinkable and, consequently, Boaz became angry as well as apprehensive.

"Lord, why after so long when I find the love of my life, the woman of my dreams, the best thing that's ever happened to me, are you taking her away. I can't even consider the loss of someone who has become so precious to me and besides we are not long married. Hasn't Naomi suffered enough bereavement? How could she face another tragedy? How can I suffer it? What do you expect of us?"

Looking up to the heavens, and wailing from deep within his soul, Boaz sounded like Naomi, all those years ago, when she'd questioned the Almighty in Moab after the unexpected loss of her loved ones.

"I've done everything you've asked of me, so why, Lord? Why would you take my beautiful Ruth away from me and away from this bereft world which needs her goodness and grace so much?" a broken Boaz enquired of God.

Professing his love for Ruth over and over again, he wept like a baby, until suddenly there could be heard the sound of laughter. It was the laughter of both Naomi and Ruth inside the home. How on earth could they laugh at such a solemn moment?

Were they mocking Boaz?

What was going on?

He'd allowed them space to pray for Ruth, not to laugh together or poke fun at him. His pride prickled, Boaz stormed inside the home and demanded answers. His face like thunder, and his emotions upside down, he only calmed down when he noticed the peaceful and even joyful expressions of both Naomi and Ruth.

Now it was Naomi's turn to leave the house to give Ruth time to explain to her troubled husband why there was so much joy in the midst of sickness and previously sorrow. Amid uncertainty and fear, God was about to birth a blessing.

"Everything is fine; your wife will explain all," Naomi reassured Boaz, caressing his shoulder as she departed, smiling kindly at him.

Then, taking the hand of Boaz and gazing dreamingly into his eyes, Ruth gestured to her husband to come closer, to hear the groundbreaking news. Nervously he leaned over and heard his wife gently whisper, "We're going to have a baby, Boaz."

"A baby, a baby," beamed Boaz.

The feeling became too much for him, and suddenly the man whose name means "strength" collapsed with a sense of great joy and relief into his wife's arms asking both her and God to forgive him for his lack of faith and trust in the Lord to bless their home.

"Even after all these years, I still can't fully trust the Lord, and yet I should have known better. He has never let me down and is such a faithful and merciful God."

"You do trust the Lord, Boaz. You are one of the most trusting, righteous and good men I've ever known."

"No, Ruth, you don't understand, while I was outside, I was shouting at God and accusing him of taking you away from me when all the time he was adding to our family and making life better."

"It's only natural, Boaz, you were just concerned about me and that's why I love you so much. You are such a wonderful husband to me."

Ruth knew how to speak to the King inside her husband, not to the shepherd boy.

Unlike many women in the town, who regularly criticised their husbands, Ruth was different. She continually praised him, and Boaz duly responded to her words of affirmation rather than any words of condemnation. She'd learned this trick from Naomi, who in their early years in Moab, regularly encouraged Elimelech, also, even though he wasn't living or acting anything like a king. Suddenly Ruth beamed the brightest of smiles, and the couple embraced for what seemed like hours until finally Ruth broke the beautiful silence between them.

"Not only has he always been with you, Boaz, but our God has also led both Naomi and me here for this very moment. I believe our baby will be great in the sight of the Lord and time will prove his place in history."

"You are so right, Ruth. Is it possible to feel this happy?" askcd a blissful Boaz.

"Yes, it is, because I feel and share in this happiness, too," replied Ruth.

Naomi stood at the entrance of the home and watched them hold each other, which brought tears to her eyes and, with it, memories of years before when her sweetheart Elimelech celebrated the births of their two sons in precisely the same way.

They were just as in love back then. The world was their oyster and the sky the limit. Where had the years gone? They had slipped through her fingers in seconds. There had been good times and bad times, which is what marriage is all about, ups and downs, highs and lows, and now that journey would belong to her cherished daughter in law Ruth and her besotted husband, Boaz.

Naomi had believed nothing could ever be salvaged or restored from the tragedies she'd encountered. But right there, the unexpected birth of another child proved her so wrong.

Through this exceptional birth, Naomi's name, family line, and heritage were miraculously restored. God had not forgotten his child Naomi. She was still the apple of his eye, and He had found a beautiful way to help heal her broken heart and restore her battered faith. He, more than anyone, had made a way where there was no way.

And so, the "miracle baby" was eventually born — a boy named Obed, meaning "a servant" — and no ordinary birth for numerous reasons.

The Bible records it like this; *"Then Naomi took the child and laid him on her bosom, and became a nurse to him. Also, the neighbour women gave him a name, saying, 'There is a son born to Naomi.' And they called his name Obed; He is the father of Jesse, the father of David."* (Ruth 4:16-17)

The gospel writer didn't fail to see the significance of Ruth's presence in the lineage of the Messiah (Matthew 1:5), and the birth of Obed is marked as extraordinary when he is recorded as the ancestor of Jesus in the book of Luke.

Think about it! A son born to a Moabite woman became the grandfather of Israel's greatest king. If this doesn't shake our all too often "prejudicial religious convictions," nothing will.

But what else does this birth highlight? Yahweh's purpose is often fullfilled through the lives of ordinary but faithful individuals like Boaz, Ruth and Naomi. Ruth had birthed a son, through whom thousands and myriads were born to God; and in being the lineal ancestor of Christ, she was instrumental in the happiness of all that shall be saved by him; even of us Gentiles, as well as those of Jewish descent.

Ruth is a witness for God to the Gentile world that he has not utterly forsaken them, that His love stretches beyond human-made borders and divisions and, in due time, strangers like Ruth could become one with God's chosen people, and partakers of his salvation.

However, not only had a man from Israel, Boaz and a foreign woman from Moab, Ruth, produced a child, Naomi's life, too, found fulfilment again through this unlikely birth.

Because of the grace of God, and the arrival of Obed, all Naomi's problems had been resolved to bring her life to a glorious and happy conclusion. Herein Ruth is the second redeemer in our story — a hidden redeemer.

By Ruth's faithfulness and excellent character, Naomi's circumstances were reversed, and her complaints were answered. Naomi had lost everything, but using Ruth, God was giving her it all back again   and more!

What am I saying!

God is a restoring God! He renewed all of their lives through their daughter in law but once Ruth gives birth to Obed, she is described as being better to Naomi than seven sons. The women and their neighbours of the town acknowledged this and announced it for the world to hear; *"Thy daughter in law, which loveth thee, is better to thee than seven sons."* (Ruth 4:15)

What an astounding declaration it is to say that Ruth "is better than seven sons" in a book in which the birth of a son is the all-consuming need! No wonder that from that moment forward, Naomi loved and cared for Obed throughout the rest of her days causing her to Praise the Lord.

"Thank you, Lord, thank you for never leaving me alone, even in those dark times in Moab, thank you for proving such a faithful God to me. Thank you for taking care of not only me but also Ruth and Boaz."

This remarkable story highlights clearly how God is not just to be celebrated in material advantages. So often we want to tell others about what God gave us, rather than what God means to us. Not so, Ruth and Boaz or Naomi. They all thanked God from the bottom of their hearts, but not for physical things; instead, they praised God for each other and God's incredible faithfulness and goodness towards them.

They were people more interested in family success than material success. It left Naomi cuddling Obed daily like he was her own: "Isn't he so cute?" she would repeat over and over again. Boaz knew he had forfeited his firstborn to become an heir to another man's family, and he knew, too, that Obed had been half-kidnapped by the doting Naomi, but it didn't matter at all to him. His life was perfect, and God was at the centre of it all.

Observing Naomi, Boaz remarked: "Look at her, she is so smitten."

"Never again will she be called Mara, never again will she feel empty, never again will she feel as though God is against her and has afflicted her."

"It is true, Boaz, what a wonderful remark", replied an astonished Ruth.

All babies bring joy to a household, of course, but this one heralded exceeding joy after what had been an excessively long night, particularly for both Naomi and Ruth.

Ruth couldn't ever recall feeling so joyful and content. Naomi, too, was ecstatic. She'd lost her family and home some years ago, but now God was restoring to her things she had assumed were lost forever. It suddenly occurred to Naomi how this boy would be adequately schooled in the ways of God and raised by a man who loved God and more than this, a man who served God with all his heart.

Naomi's new little cutie pie soon became quite the treasure in the town of Bethlehem at that time. Grandmas' boy had both Naomi and the city fawning all over him. Every stage of his life was greeted with prophecies by the people of the town who regularly gathered to check on his progress, yet they had no idea of just how significant this baby would ultimately become the father of Jesse, who was the father of the great King David; that same little boy who would one day topple the great Goliath.

"May God use this baby in a mighty way?"

"Blessed be the Lord, which hath not left thee this day without a kinsman, and may the Lord make his name famous in Israel."

"May he be unto you a restorer of life and let him restore everything that the enemy took from you in your old age and in ways you will never believe."

Naomi marvelled at such prophecies, and her heart leapt with sheer joy and excitement. Of course, Obed wasn't Naomi's; he belonged to Ruth and Boaz, but there was no denying the fact that Naomi finally had a grandson, a next-of-kin, and an all-important man in her life.

Remember, her story began with the loss of the men in her life but ended with her cradling her newest little male relative in her arms. God may not always give us back what we lost in the same way, but Naomi is proof that He does restore in his time and in His unique way.

In Ruth's generation, a man symbolised security, so Naomi was pleased as punch by the arrival of this baby boy; moreover, Naomi's friends named the child Obed, meaning 'servant' or 'workman', a unique and special baby if ever there was one being the father of the great King David and a remarkable birth in history.

There have, of course, been many other outstanding births, from Moses to Obed to the Apostle Paul, from Martin Luther King, to Bill Gates, William Shakespeare, Nelson Mandela, Albert Einstein, Christopher Columbus, Ernest Hemmingway, Eleanor Roosevelt, Rosa Parks, Malala Yousafzai, Helen Keller, the list is endless.

Yet there has never been a birth like the birth of Jesus!

His delivery was no normal birth. Like any baby, Jesus was beautiful, but for many reasons, His was no ordinary birth. Jesus was born of a virgin and without sin. No other baby in history, not Moses, Obed or Paul, was born in this way. The Bible states; *"Behold, a virgin shall be with child and shall bring forth a son, and they shall call his name Emmanuel, which being interpreted is, God with us."* (Matthew 1:23)

The Bible's narrative about the Virgin Mary and the birth of Jesus is not a legend — not at all.

Instead, the Bible's most extensive account about Mary was written by Luke, who was a physician, and therefore knew that the virgin birth of Jesus was no ordinary birth but also impossible apart from God. Jesus was born of a virgin: to show that he was sent into the world by God. Thus, His was no ordinary birth. He was no ordinary human being! He wasn't just another man — not even a great one. He was God in human flesh, sent from heaven to save us from our sins. As the angel told Joseph, *"Do not be afraid to take Mary home as your wife. ...She will give birth to a son, and you are to give him the name Jesus (which means 'the Lord saves'), because he will save his people from their sins."* (Matthew 1:20-21)

But something else, which makes the birth of Jesus amazing; He came to make a way where there is no way. Jesus Christ Himself proclaims in John's Gospel; *"I am the way, the truth, and the life: no man cometh unto the Father, but by me."* (John 14:6)

No other prophet, person or God made such a claim. Jesus has made way for us to have direct access to the Father, to Almighty God! No one else has ever accomplished this, not Boaz, or Ruth who themselves are pictures of redemption, not Naomi, a description of survival — only Jesus has done this. Notwithstanding; Ruth is still a wonderful picture of a redeemer to Naomi.

Remember how Naomi went seeking a better life back in Bethlehem? She had told Ruth and Orpah to return to Moab to their family, friends, wealth and connections. She had pleaded with them not to emigrate with her. Orpah relented and returned but, as we know, Ruth refused to leave her mother in laws side. Naomi had expected a better and more blessed life, but not Ruth. Ruth is extraordinary not just because of the great loyalty she showed to Naomi, but Ruth had anticipated a worse life in Bethlehem. You will never read of any immigrant who went in search of a worse life, except for Ruth.

Similarly, lots of people today accept Jesus, assuming they are signing up for a better life, and in many cases, this can be true, but there are thousands of persecuted and suffering Christians who have experienced a worse life here on earth to win the crown of eternal life with God in heaven. Like Moses, who left the glory of Egypt and became a Hebrew slave who would ultimately deliver the people of God, so, too, Ruth chose persecution above prestige. She knew if she remained in Moab where her prospects materially were much better with family and a husband to care for her, then her faith would die as a result,

She had to go where the people of God resided to find her purpose and destiny. It was a huge gamble, but one she simply had to take. Ruth also perceived that if she returned with Orpah leaving Naomi alone, then her mother in law wouldn't survive, but if she made the ultimate sacrifice and followed her then Naomi would not perish, a picture of the compassion and love of our great Redeemer, the Lord Jesus Christ, who knowing his destiny, gave up the splendour of heaven to redeem us on the cross at Calvary, who has promised never to leave us or forsake us. If Ruth and Naomi were to get their lives back; then Ruth had concluded she would have to throw away her security. If Naomi's family name was to be retrieved, then Ruth would have to sacrifice her family. In other words, she impoverished herself so Naomi could become rich. In precisely the same way the bible says of Jesus; "*Who, being in the form of God, thought it not robbery to be made equal with*

God: But made himself of no reputation, and took upon him the form of a servant, and was made in the likeness of men. And being found in the fashion of men he humbled himself and became obedient unto death, even the death of the cross." (Philippians 2:6-8)

Naomi, bereaved of her husband and two sons suddenly holds this new child, the son of Ruth and Boaz, becoming part of a family again, with a loving and fulfilling role to play.

God would and did restore everything that was stolen from Naomi's life. He would heal every hurt and every pain. God is a restoring God!

And, so as she sat there in a Bethlehem field, looking over the beautiful landscape, and reflecting on all that God had done, her eyes welled up with tears for this unusual and special birth, for a gift retrieved, a love restored and life reborn.

Sixteen

Restored

"And I will restore to you the years that the locust hath eaten,
the cankerworm, and the caterpillar, and the palmerworm,
my great army which I sent among you." (Joel 2:25)

As Naomi stood up, with Obed in her arms facing the beautiful background of Israel, her mind began to drift again to all she'd endured.

Over twenty years had passed since that momentous moment when they'd emigrated and left a place they'd been brought up in favour of the land of Moab. Now she had returned and was standing on the familiar ground, yet her life flashed before her as one extraordinary journey.

Following her departure from Israel, she recalled how they'd experienced the "best of times" and the "worst of times" as they all sampled new things, meeting new people and getting fresh opportunities, but she winced, too, recalling how she'd struggled immensely to adapt to her new environment. No financial security in Moab had brought added pressures, and the loss of her general identity had proved an enormous challenge.

Then it occurred to Naomi that what she'd missed more than anything was the family of God she'd known. The friendships she'd made, and her family ties were much stronger than she had imagined and, so, as we've read, Naomi endured a phase, unlike anything she'd experienced previously.

Now older and wiser, of course, it became apparent to her how much she'd learned about life, love and herself. Cuddling her little bundle of joy, Obed, Naomi knew that it is possible to make a life-changing decision, and then by the grace of God, survive.

The consequences came and went, but through it all, God remained faithful to his child. She had come to appreciate her former brethren, place of worship and her specific role in society.

In those years of isolation in Moab, Naomi was required, on many occasions, to depend solely on God and the kindness of others. She understood the phrase "When God is all you have, God is all you need." Many times when Naomi thought she would go under, God stepped in and made a way where there didn't seem to be one.

Notwithstanding; those years in the wilderness were an extraordinarily lonely and long night full of sorrow and despair. Any familiarity she might have felt towards Israel and her people before the move to Moab, would, by now, have been entirely erased.

If anyone ever appreciated what God had blessed them with, namely a great family, place of worship and place in society, it was Naomi.

Gazing at the beautiful countryside in front of her, she began to recall the many times she'd wondered if restoration to her previous family, place of worship and country was ever possible, and on most occasions, she'd laughed it off.

"There's too much water under the bridge," Naomi would often think to herself.

"Some things can't be fixed" and "it's too late for such a miracle to take place" were other excuses she'd offered.

Remember, the relationships with her brethren had only broken down due to a lack of contact and a new life far away, not because she hadn't wanted them to continue. Furthermore, it had grieved her on many occasions how she'd lost touch with people she'd spent so many years with previously; people this pleasant lady regarded as her family members. There was an ache in her heart at being separated from them, especially her loved ones and those she'd served alongside in ministry, who'd become so dear to her. Suddenly she was confronted with the goodness of God and His fantastic restoration in her life. Looking out at God's handiwork of creation in front of her, dazzled by the magnificence of the mountains and the depths of the valleys, for the first time Naomi realised how her life had recovered because of the love of something as small as a newborn child.

The seasons had changed but through it all God had stayed faithful. God had restored everything that was stolen from her life. He had healed every hurt and every pain.

Despite her losses, she would love and cherish Obed for the rest of her days as if he was her own. So, at that moment, an overwhelming sense of God's goodness and presence surrounded her causing her to thank the Lord over and over again for His faithfulness towards her and her family. Boaz wasn't there and neither was Ruth. Now, in the plains of Israel, it was just Naomi and her God. She looked back and marvelled at how far she'd travelled but didn't wonder anymore how she'd made it. Naomi already knew the answer; only by the grace of God had she made it through. For without God's help and His strength, she could have done nothing. Reflecting, too, on the loyalty of her daughter in law, Ruth, and her part in all this restoration, Naomi gained the most significant lesson of her life, and one she would never forget — *friendship is the first key to recovery.*

Friendship

When the apostle Paul and Barnabas separated during their ministry, they lost friendship and something of what they'd enjoyed because two is always better than one.

Notwithstanding: God helped Paul go on to become a mighty preacher in his own right and Barnabas a wonderful encourager to the flock of God, earning him the nickname "Son of consolation." Notably, however, the Bible also appears to indicate that the breakdown of the relationship between these two Christian evangelists, while seemingly allowed in the purpose of God, was mended before they died.

God hates to see friendships and relationships between brethren damaged.

True brethren and genuine friendship will always seek a way back. God is ultimately a restoring God and a God of unity, and he delights to see his people "singing from the same hymn sheet," as it were. Unity and restoration are God's speciality and the place where his blessing most dwells. If you don't feel the blessing of God right now, check out your relationships. Are there any of God's people you are at variance with?

The Bible reminds us; *"Behold, how good and how pleasant it is for brethren to dwell together in unity! It is like the precious ointment upon the head, that ran down upon the beard, even Aaron's beard: that went down to the skirts of his garments; As the dew of Hermon, and as the dew that descended upon the mountains of Zion: for there the Lord commanded the blessing, even life for evermore."* (Psalm 133)

It appears God is not as interested in restoring our business and material situations, even our ministerial positions, as He is in rebuilding our friendships and relationships with our brethren. Notice how Naomi's restoration didn't arrive by economic programmes etc. or by talent or ability in some area, instead, it came by deep lasting friendship.

The name Ruth in Hebrew has two meanings: One is a friend, and the other is beauty. Put these together, and you get "Beautiful friend." Of course, Ruth had already become a beautiful friend to Naomi; now she had become a lover and friend to her devoted husband, Boaz. Ruth changed the lives of both Naomi (a grief-stricken widow) and Boaz (a wealthy, but lonely landowner) due to her capacity for friendship.

Do we realise how powerful friendships are?

Friendships change people's lives and lead to a restoration of astonishing proportions.

Are you struggling because a once beautiful friendship has broken down? Making every effort to restore it will replace pride and bitterness with peace and unity.

Preaching is good, but friendship is powerful. We conquer the world as friends but accomplish nothing as strangers. The Bible declares; *"One shall chase a thousand but two shall put ten thousand to flight."* (Deuteronomy 32:30)

Some try to navigate their way through life alone; uncomfortable making friends, even though God has ordained us to walk the journey of life together. He has assigned people to help us reach our destiny, as He did with Naomi and Boaz.

The reason why Naomi missed her homeland and people so much is because they were, and still are, the people God intended her to have. How we connect and interact with others can often serve as a sign that we are not only in the right place but also in the will of God. Still, some maintain they don't need friends or anyone so long as they have Jesus.

"He alone is all we need" they claim, something which sounds spiritual, but no man is an island! We all need friendships. We are created to communicate with God first and then others, especially those God has assigned to our lives. Imagine if Naomi had never met Ruth, or if Ruth had never met Naomi? Imagine if they both hadn't come across a wealthy kinsman named Boaz? It begs an important question: Could a lack of essential friendships be the missing link in your life right now?

You can't be respected if you're not connected.

Friendship is the first key to your restoration.

Family

Another vital component in finding restoration is finding the right family, and we see this especially in the story of Naomi, Ruth and Boaz. In fact, Ruth removes, in her story, the myth that unless we have the perfect family, we cannot have the perfect ending.

Many families are dysfunctional today which is why God in His mercy and wisdom gave us another family — the family of God. Some people are blessed with a good earthly family, but many others are not, yet that is not the end. The good news is we are not family only by our natural blood type, but with God, we are family through the blood of Jesus. By accepting Jesus Christ into our hearts, we become part of what is known as "the family of God." This family allows for restoration of incredible proportions and includes people from every tribe and tongue.

For example, Ruth broke through cultural barriers which suggested that unless a family had sons, no blessing would follow. She also became a part of the covenant of Jesus Christ despite beginning her life in the heathen land of Moab. And, as we've read, the Bible even describes Ruth as being "better than seven sons" to Naomi.

The grace of God can make up to you anything you may have lost, or didn't have in the first place, and His grace has the power to break any negative cycle in your life?

Your blessing may not come in the same way you experienced it previously, but the grace of God can still restore, and His divinely appointed relationships in your life are more powerful than the perfect family.

Mephibosheth is a man we read about in the second book of Samuel? He was lame on his feet from the age of five, but ultimately rescued by King David in Lodebar, a location described as "a place of nothing," but eventually David helped restore him to the King's table and his former status. Because of an oath between David and Saul's son, Jonathan, David remained concerned for Mephibosheth and went looking for him.

Like Jesus, who left the ninety-nine sheep and went after the missing one, David also shows the supreme heart of shepherd by searching for his long-lost relative to have him restored to his former position. The Bible says in the second book of Samuel that David asked; *"Is there yet any that is left of the house of Saul, that I may show him kindness for Jonathan's sake?"* (2 Samuel 9:1)

It is said that after the word love, kindness is the most beautiful word in the world. There are many of God's greatest servants today living in Lodebar, the place of no pasture, prospects or provision, left feeling forgotten and rejected. All of them require the kindness David offered to Mephibosheth, the grandson of King Saul, a man destined at one time to become king, until everything changed following a terrible accident when he was young leaving him paralysed for life.

He wasn't born lame, but to be a king, yet events changed his destiny.

Is this you?

Are you born for greatness, born to be a king, but events have derailed your dream and held up your destiny?

Have you been rerouted from your life's purpose?

Do things look so different to how you had imagined they would turn out?

If you are in such a place, perhaps a David is on his way to haste your restoration plan.

Like Naomi, Mephibosheth spent years in exile and isolation. His dreams shattered, all hope was gone, and no one would have offered him a prayer of recovery. After his father Jonathan and grandfather Saul died, he drifted and merely existed for many years in Lodebar, which also means the place of no fruit. A forgotten man, and a rejected saint, he felt hopeless but when we're down to nothing, God is usually up to something.

Mephibosheth had endured the place of nothing for years until God stepped in using the tender-hearted and concerned David. The family ties between Saul and Mephibosheth and the deep friendship between David and Jonathan meant nothing could destroy their great bond, not even the death of Jonathan. What am I saying! God can turn the most horrendous of situations in our favour and will often use someone like David to make it happen.

He knows how to bless in a mess. The stronger our pain, the higher the purpose! All God needs is to get us to the right place and send us the right person so the miraculous can materialise.

At first, Mephibosheth was frightened, but David puts him at ease with the words; *"I will surely show you kindness for the sake of your father, Jonathan. I will restore to you all the land that belonged to your grandfather Saul, and you will always eat at my table."* (2 Samuel 2:7)

The question is, of course, why did David feel such an obligation and desire to restore Mephibosheth? No one else cared about a lame man who had disappeared from public life years ago, so why David? He was a King and needed nothing. It is because David had made an oath and had a love for his brethren, but remember, he had also experienced the grace and mercy of God in his life, so if anyone understood the agony of "falling out of fellowship" or "becoming lame on one's feet", spiritually speaking, of course, it was David.

Rarely has there been such a public ministerial humiliation as his, yet, God restored David completely. He received forgiveness for his adultery with Bathsheba and his part in the murder of her husband.

What's remarkable is the fact that this great King who is referred to as *"a man after God's own heart"* wrote the majority of his best work after his fall, and not before, proving that any form of failure is not the end.

Abraham Lincoln is recalled as one of America's great presidents. What people forget, however, is the number of failures he experienced in his life — failure in business, he suffered a nervous breakdown, he was defeated for public office, including standing for the Senate and Vice President. Yet he ultimately became a great president.

Who told you it's over?

Who said God can't use you again?

God's restoration, mercy and grace are more magnificent than the worst weapon of the enemy.

David knew all about God's restoring power, and he also knew how merciful God is.

True, sadly there were consequences following David's fall when his young child with Bathsheba died, but God graciously restored to them another son called Solomon and the Bible records how God loved him.

In Psalm 51 David asked God, *"Restore unto me the joy of my salvation."* (Psalm 51:12)

Then at the beginning of the chapter he states; *"Have mercy upon me, O God, according to thy loving-kindness: according unto the multitude of thy tender mercies blot out my transgressions."* (Psalm 51:1), but in Psalm 23 he added the words; *"He restores my soul, he leads me in the paths of righteousness for his name's sake."* (Psalm 23:3)

It is one thing to hear about a restoring God, but quite another to experience Him for oneself and, like David, once we do we will never be the same again. Until broken in the same way as David we cannot understand the pain of others who slip and fall, nor understand the importance of family to restoration.

Mephibosheth, therefore, is a picture of beautiful redemption available to those who come humbly before the King of kings; Jesus Christ Who offers all of us a chance to eat at the King's table forever. Even if we have nothing to bring, or have experienced shame and defeat, whether we are young or old, handicapped or sick, we are offered a royal inheritance just like Mephibosheth.

Like King David, many people today are suffering from poor life choices or simply from undeserved incidents which have seen them lose everything. They don't require a lecture or judgement because they're undoubtedly already well aware of what led to their current adverse circumstances. Instead, they need genuine love and compassion from the family of God. God desires for us to help restore any fallen brethren, whether they have fallen through sin, bad choices or been affected by unfortunate life circumstances. Jesus said to Simon Peter; *"But I have prayed for thee, that thy faith fail not: and when thou art converted, strengthen thy brethren."* (Luke 22:32). Paul adds; *"Bear ye one another's burdens, and so fulfil the law of Christ."* (Galatians 6:2)

The law of Christ is a law of love and restoration, which rejoices in the elevation and recovery of his people, not a harsh law that delights in their ultimate downfall.

In the same way, David, Naomi, Ruth and Boaz may have lived in Old Testament times, but they clearly understood the grace of God and the power of restorative grace. They were people of indisputable love and compassion and tremendous faith.

Faith

And, so, our story concludes with the third component to restoration — faith.

Remember, Naomi had looked back with regret at many unfortunate incidents in her life, she'd experienced numerous wasted years, but she never stopped trusting God to deliver her and replace the man factor in her life. Ruth 4 records; *"And he shall be unto you a restorer of thy life and a nourisher of thine old age."* (Ruth 4:16)

Through God's restorative power, the faith of Naomi was rewarded, and her prayers were answered. In the same way, Ruth needed to show exceptional faith leaving her homeland and following a woman from another culture who served another god, "but without faith" the Bible says; *"it is impossible to please Him (God) for he that comes to God must believe that he is and that he is a rewarder of those who diligently seek him."* (Hebrews 11:6)

Both women had lost their husbands and livelihoods, but God still came through for them restoring everything through Boaz and his inheritance. If God can restore to Naomi her name, family line, and heritage, even her life what can He do for you?

The prophet Joel declared; *"And I will restore to you the years that the locust hath eaten, the cankerworm, and the caterpillar, and the palmerworm, my great army which I sent among you."* (Joel 2:25)

In other words, in God's hands, nothing is wasted, and He can restore any lost cause. Consider when Jesus took five loaves of bread and three fish and fed over five thousand people, he said; *"Gather up now the fragments (the broken pieces that are left over) so that nothing may be lost or wasted."* (John 6:12)

Do you feel your life wasted?

Maybe you believe it's too late to recover what you've lost?

Then God has a word for you. If you gather up the fragments of your life and lay them before the Lord, He will restore and rebuild the broken areas of your life because God cares about the particles and pieces.

The prodigal son in Luke 15 believed he'd wasted his life by spending his inheritance, but when he brought the fragments and pieces of his life back to his father, his father completely restored what seemed wasted.

In the same way, our heavenly Father wants to do the same. He repairs and restores every broken life and dream.

John wrote; *"The thief comes not but for to steal, kill and destroy, but I am come that ye might have life and that they might have it more abundantly."* (John 10:10), while Isaiah the prophet adds; *"Those from among you shall build the old waste places; you shall raise up the foundations of many generations; And you shall be called the repairer of the breach and the restorer of streets to dwell."* (Isaiah 58:12)

To those who are still waiting to see unsaved loved ones come to know the Lord, do not stop praying because God wastes nothing.

Here is where we meet our third redeemer and great restorer, Jesus.

Remember Boaz was the first redeemer, being a kinsman and paying a debt they couldn't pay. Ruth the second redeemer sacrificing everything for others, but in Jesus, we see the restoring redeemer. Just as Boaz Jesus paid a debt, we couldn't pay to forgive us of our sins. Like Ruth, He left His Father's throne above to come down to this sinful world. And in the same way, Boaz and Ruth became one flesh, Christ has made us part of His covenant and brought us into the family of God. Ruth was a foreigner, childless, and a widow who was left in complete poverty with no source of support. Nevertheless, Ruth finally accepted the gospel and joined the Lord's covenant people.

John records; *"Behold what manner of love the Father hath bestowed upon us, that we should be called the sons of God."* (1 John 3:1)

Though she couldn't deliver herself from her destitute condition, she was ultimately "redeemed" by her kinsman Boaz, a man of Bethlehem. Due to her faith-driven actions and the kindness of her redeemer, Ruth married again, was fully accepted as an Israelite, became a woman of some wealth, and ended up blessed with children.

God had helped her recover much of what she'd lost!

Even when the great King David endured the terrible experiences of having his two wives kidnapped, his stuff taken and seeing the village of Ziglag destroyed by fire, he was informed by God that he would recover all — which he did. The first book of Samuel records; *"And David recovered all that the Amalekites had carried away and David rescued his two wives."* (1 Samuel 30:20)

God is a restoring God!

The life of Naomi teaches us many lessons in this story, especially about God's restoring power and His amazing desire to replace what was taken, but the experience of Ruth is: we cannot save ourselves, but must rely on a redeemer from Bethlehem, One who can lift us from our fallen state and restore us as part of His family.

And here is the most remarkable news: The book of Ruth reminds us that the great-grandmother of the revered King David was a faithful woman from Moab called Ruth.

Even Jesus, the redeemer of Israel and all humanity, was one of Ruth's descendants. (Matthew 1:5-16). Is this why Ruth uttered those amazing words, *"may nothing but death part me from you,"* for Jesus our restorer also said, *"I will never leave thee or forsake thee but I will be with you always even unto the end of the world."* (Hebrews 3:5)

Some believe if we sin badly, enough God turns His back on us. Jesus said the opposite. He came to redeem us and forgive sins and restore lives.

Restoration is what He does best!

Remember, the apostle Peter denied the Lord publically, but was restored less than forty days after the resurrection. God is a restoring God!

And Jesus is the greatest friend of all; even greater than Ruth who was prepared to die for Naomi. In fact, the greatest redeemer is neither Ruth nor Boaz as impressive as they were; the greatest redeemer is Jesus because only he can save the souls of humanity and put the broken lives of people back together.

Only Christ redeems from sin and brokenness; there is no other god or saviour who can restore like Him and display such mercy. Naomi is given another man-child to nurse, love and care for and God restored to her years she thought were unredeemable. Initially Naomi and Ruth had given up their lives for God's will, but God spectacularly replaced what they'd lost previously.

Naomi found restoration from a loving heavenly father; she found a fresh song in her heart again and a reason to rejoice. She could indeed say like the women in Isaiah; *"Sing, O barren, thou that didst not bear; break forth into singing, and cry aloud, thou that didst not travail with child: for more are the children of the desolate than the children of the married wife, saith the LORD."* (Isaiah 54:1)

What is the central message of the story of Naomi? Why is her story worth recalling and worth examining carefully? It is that God will restore everything we've lost, but not necessarily in the way, we might have expected. He restores in His time and in His purpose, allowing us to live and laugh again. Yes, above all else, Naomi is proof that God's mysterious kindness always gives us back what we lost, accompanied by incredible wisdom and beautiful memories.

Epilogue

The story complete, David sat mesmerised.

His grandfather could see he was impressed and deep in thought. "If your great grandmother and Naomi had not believed in God through their hard times, none of us may be sitting here today."

David nodded in agreement at the words of his grandfather, but could God come through for him in the same supernatural way?

That was the burning question inside him.

Recognising the excitement within David, his grandfather added, "Do you recall how God helped you to fight off a lion and a bear that was attacking your land? Listen to me, David, the same God will now help you to overcome your enemies and become King."

As the old man continued speaking, he lost sight of David for a moment, and then noticed that his grandson was no longer sitting there.

Where had he gone?

He was there a few seconds ago.

When he looked up, he saw something that warmed his heart, the sight of a rejuvenated young David marching confidently towards the middle of the field.

He appeared a different person.

His head was up, and his shoulders were square.

David stopped abruptly and aimed at the same tree he had failed to hit earlier, but this time there was no mistake, it was a bulls-eye.

His focus had returned, and David knew it.

The young boy glanced back towards his grandfather and smiled at him before sending him a cheeky little wink. With that, he turned and walked up the hill towards the battlefield, a man on a mission, armed and anointed, he was now ready to face the mighty Goliath.